Reggae Bloodlines

In Search Of The Music And Culture Of Jamaica

Text by
Stephen Davis

Photographs by
Peter Simon

ANCHOR·PRESS·DOUBLEDAY

The Anchor Books edition is the first publication of *Reggae Bloodlines* Anchor Books edition: 1977.

Permission to excerpt song lyrics is granted by the following: "Slave Driver," 1972, Tuff Gong Music Ltd.; "Johnnie Too Bad," 1971, Ackee Music Inc.; "Shanty Town," 1971, Irving Music Ltd.; "No Chuck It," 1975, Ackee Music Inc.; "Them Belly Full," 1974, Tuff Gong Music Ltd.; "Small Ax," 1973, Tuff Gong Music Ltd.; "Jah Live," 1975, Tuff Gong Music Ltd.; "Book of Rules," 1976, Ackee Music Inc.; "Black Star Liners," 1976, Fred Locks Music Ltd.; "Blackheart Man," 1976, Solomonic Music; "Right Time," 1976, Virgin Music Ltd.; "Legalize It," Peter Tosh, © 1975 No. 11 Music, 5112 Hollywood Blvd.; Los Angeles, CA 90027; "Pressure Drop," F. Hibbert, © 1972 Sheila Music. All rights for the U.S. and Canada, controlled by No. 11 Music (BMI), 5112 Hollywood Blvd., Los Angeles, CA 90027.

Library of Congress Catalog Card Number 76–42428
ISBN: 0-385-12330-2
Text copyright © 1977 by Stephen Davis
Photographs copyright © 1977 by Peter Simon
All Rights Reserved
Printed in the United States of America
First Edition

PHOTO CREDITS

KIM GOTTLIEB; pp. 15, 36, 37 (top), 39, 42 (bottom), 43, 47 (top), 56, 68, 74, 90, 105, 110, 113, 117, 138
DENNIS MORRIS; pp. 33 (bottom), 34, 59 (top), 89, 97, 105, 115, 144 (top), 145 (right)
JAMAICAN TOURIST BOARD; p. 10
COURTESY OF MICHAEL OCHS ARCHIVE; facing page 1, pp. 2, 16, 88 (left)
DAVID BURNETT; pp. 44, 45, 46 (bottom), 59 (bottom)
SUSAN WEINIK; p. 62
CLIVE WILLIAMS; p. 209
JAMES VANDERZEE; p. 66
DAVID CHANDLER; p. 79

Design: Robert Aulicino

When you're out in the country, in the old estates, and you see the country people walking to church or rocking in their hammocks or drinking in the little bars, you don't think it's that kind of country. But every country is that kind of country.

V. S. NAIPAUL
Guerrillas

Acknowledgments

This book is indebted to dozens of friends in Jamaica, Britain, and the States. The authors extend heartfelt thanks to: Howard Greenberg, who opened more doors than we could walk through; Neville Gallimore, M.P., who opened a few more; The Hon. Michael Manley; Valentine Lindo; Ken Chen Young; Jeff Walker of Island Records, who was generous with his patience and the very Dread mushroom elixir; Velma of the Sutton Place Hotel, Kingston; Don Williams, who compiled the discography and helped with the interviewing; photographers Dennis Morris, Kim Gottlieb, and Dave Burnett; the legendary Ed "Rootsman" Kritzler, the best friend an emerging nation ever had and one of the last of the Ravers; Earl Chin; Jude Arons; Ronni Berman; Karl Frederich of Coconut Cove, Negril; Mike Ochs, who maintains a valuable reggae archive; Christopher Davis; Jacqueline Entwhistle; Roy Pace; Luke Erlich, the "White Ram," who read the text and straightened it out here and there; Danny Schecter of WBCN-FM, Boston; and Marie Dutton Brown of Anchor Press, who put up with us and paid the rent.

Portions of this book were published in somewhat different form in the New York *Times Magazine* and *New Age*.

Contents

Jimmy Cliff as Ivan O. Martin

① Introduction

. . . a good part of the attraction of reggae music to its metropolitan audience is the anger and protest of the lyrics. We obviously face a contradiction between the message of urban poverty and protest which reggae conveys and that of pleasure and relaxation inherent in our holiday product.

In short, when we promote reggae music we are promoting an aspect of Jamaican culture which is bound to draw attention to some of the harsher circumstances of our lives. All the articles written on the sound so far do this. Our view is that we should leave other agencies and local music interests to carry the ball from here on.

—*from a Jamaica Tourist Board memorandum*
October 10, 1975

Clearly, then, reggae is subversive and dangerous and perhaps ought to be forbidden. Reggae is outlaw music, primitive and tribal. Reggae is hypnotic, trance music. Zero-degree music. A cultural shock wave emanating from the Caribbean, just ninety miles south of Cuba. And as a matter of fact, reggae music *is* forbidden to a certain extent in its homeland, Jamaica. Some of the more militant and aggressive singles (like "Jah Kingdom Go to Waste" and Max Romeo's succinct "War in a Babylon") have been banned from the air as the worried Jamaican Government tries to keep an uneasy truce between warring political factions by keeping inflammatory reggae off the radio. Reggae is ghetto music, the sound of the slums, and only gets ghetto air time in Jamaica—usually between midnight and dawn, when most Jamaicans are sleeping. By day the island's two stations blast out glossy American disco records that go down like Pablum or formula.

But somehow the progress of reggae and Jamaican music is incredible, unprecedented, totally unpredicted (except in Jamaica, where for years they've been saying that their music would take over the world). If you said ten years ago that one of the dominant international musical forces of the Seventies would be Kingstonian ghetto music, you would've been called an idiot or worse. Yet reggae made it, is making it, and it's too late to stop now.

From a synthesis of various soul musics and African and Afro-Caribbean rhythms, reggae evolved in the West Kingston slums in the mid-Sixties. Reggae songs found their way onto Jamaican radio and were picked out of the airwaves by cheap transistors on other islands. Reggae flew into London with Jamaican immigrants and holed up in a basement flat in Brixton shivering through its first northern winters. While the true reggae masters remained unknown outside of Jamaica, a Texas-born soul singer named Johnny Nash tried to get reggae going in Europe and the States around 1966, but nobody was interested. Not until Anglo-American white pop musicians picked up on the rhythms and tried, however lamely, to reproduce them did reggae start to penetrate the most difficult boundaries our nations have—our thick cultural walls. An English band called Mungo Jerry stole the beat in 1969 and suddenly had a hit single, "In the Summertime." Then Paul Simon recorded "Mother and Child Reunion" in Kingston, using local session musicians and a proto-reggae sensibility. In 1971, Johnny Nash tried again, using the style for "I Can See Clearly Now," which turned out to be a hit. Later his version of Bob Marley's "Stir It Up" became the first international reggae smash. Eric Clapton and The Rolling Stones covered reggae songs and suddenly, within the space of only a few years, reggae and reggae-derived songs moved into the repertoire of the most widely heard musicians in the world. Gradually, too slowly for some, the Jamaican reggae masters emerged from obscurity to show the pop stars and the rest what roots music is all about, the way you play it and dance to it and what happens psychophysically when humans are exposed to the thunder and sway of the real thing. And the real reggae turned out to be a new lens, bringing into sharp focus the turbulence and anguish of the little corner of the Third World called Jamaica.

Occasionally in the late Sixties an American record company would buy a reggae single that had been successful in Jamaica or England and release it in the States. The first reg-

Desmond Dekker

gae song to be played on American stations was Desmond Dekker's "Israelites," with its archetypal reggae theme: Black Africans, the metaphoric lost tribes of Israel, sold into the bondage of a Caribbean Babylon. The following year, 1969, Jimmy Cliff's dark, epistolary "Vietnam" haunted the airflow with its tough antiwar lyric and the potency of its rock-steady beat. Like "Israelites," Cliff's song had a bit of success around the country but quickly faded away.

I heard little more about reggae until the late winter of 1972, when I was in London on business. I had tea one afternoon with Charlie Gillette, a writer and BBC disc jockey, who gave me an album and suggested I play it when I had a chance. "This might interest you," Gillette said. The album was the soundtrack to *The Harder They Come*.

A month later I finally got a chance to hear the album I'd been dutifully carrying around with me. All I can say is that I was *stunned* by the stops-out funk, played by obscure but plainly brilliant Jamaicans—Jimmy Cliff, the Maytals, the Melodians, the Slickers, Scotty, and Desmond Dekker. A short while later *The Harder They Come,* produced by a Jamaican director named Perry Henzell, opened in Boston. I went to see it, like many of the film's fans, unprepared to be immersed in the dazzling, fearsome world Henzell re-creates.

Shot almost entirely in Kingston, using no professional actors, *The Harder They Come* is probably the first English language film ever to require English subtitles until the audience becomes accustomed to the thick Jamaican patois. The story is about Ivan O. Martin, a country boy who migrates to Kingston to seek his fortune as a reggae star. Soon after he gets off the bus from Bog Walk or Maggotty or whatever hill country backwater he's running from, Ivan's clothes are stolen and he finds himself penniless in the teeming city. Ivan winds up in Trench Town and is inducted into the ganja trade by a Rastafarian brother. He becomes a small-time street hustler to survive, but his fantasy is reggae godhood; he joins the pitiful lineup of aspiring musicians warbling outside the barbed-wire gates of Mr. Hilton's recording studio, vainly trying to interest the swinish producer in his song as Hilton whizzes by contemptuously in his white Mercedes.

Finally Ivan gets a chance to peek into the studio, where the Maytals happen to be rehearsing their masterpiece, "Pressure Drop."

Bull Bay

He convinces producer Hilton to let him record his song, "The Harder They Come," and the number is cut in a blistering performance by Cliff in the studio. Hilton is impressed and offers Ivan the standard reggae contract—twenty dollars for the song and no royalties. Ivan refuses indignantly at first but later relents in desperation. Hilton gives him the money but secretly orders that the song not be released. "He's a troublemaker," Hilton says of Ivan. "I don't want to build him up."

Then the pressure starts to drop on Ivan. When Preacher, Ivan's only benefactor, turns against him because Ivan has been fooling with Preacher's young protégée, one of Preacher's goons tries to steal Ivan's precious bicycle. In the most vicious and realistic knife fight ever captured on film, Ivan cuts up the goon and winds up sentenced to the whipping post, where he loses control of his bladder as the lash cuts into him.

Gradually Ivan sinks deeper into the ganja trade. He leads a revolt among the small dealers when he realizes that the ganja he is selling for two dollars is resold in the States for two hundred dollars a pound. Rather than go back to jail, he kills a policeman, wounds a woman who tries to betray him, shoots up five more cops, and generally turns into a Kingstonian Staggerlee. He chases the ganja kingpin out of Trench Town at gunpoint. In the manner of Rhygin, the legendary Jamaican bandit of the Forties, Ivan has photos taken of his flashy clothes and gunplay and sends them to the newspapers. Hilton takes advantage of Ivan's notoriety and releases "The Harder They Come," which of course soars to the top of the charts. The country bumpkin is transmogrified into both reggae star and folk hero on the bad side of the law. The ultimate reggae fantasy.

All this proves too much for the police, who close down the ganja trade until Ivan is caught. He tries to hide out, but the cops are leaning on the trade so hard that the Jamaican population becomes demoralized and Ivan's own woman goes back to Preacher to turn the rebel in. The film ends on Lime Key, where Ivan, like Rhygin the bandit, tries to jump a freighter to Cuba. He misses the boat and must swim back to the key, where the police and army are waiting for him. But Ivan O. Martin won't be taken alive. Recalling the lurid images of the Clint Eastwood spaghetti westerns so popular in Jamaica, Ivan taunts the police and tells them to send out their baddest man to draw. Ivan dies laughing.

In the few years since its release, *The Harder They Come* has become one of the longest-playing cult movies in America. The society it portrays, authentically and critically, with its hungry youth, avaricious reggae producers, manipulative police, and outrageous dope trade, proved fascinating to young people identified with Ivan's disaffection from and refusal to surrender to the grinding injustice of the System. The film injected a small dose of Jamaican culture into the thought patterns of young, hip Americans that paved the way for reggae's introduction to an international audience. Ironically *The Harder They Come* is technically banned in Jamaica under current government regulations forbidding violent movies.

The success of *The Harder They Come* propelled singer Jimmy Cliff's career. Other major Jamaican groups—the Wailers, Toots and the Maytals—have American record contracts and tour the States and Europe regularly. But down in Jamaica there are still dozens of reggae masters quietly seething as they wait for the established stars to make it abroad and open the doors a little further for them.

Photographer Peter Simon and I spent most of the winter of 1976 in Jamaica, visiting and talking with some of these reggae master musicians as well as the producers, ganja traders, Rastafarian brethren and elders, and even a politician or two; we were trying to get a line on the force that sets the reggae cosmology

Jimmy Cliff, center, Spanish Town Road

into motion and keeps it spinning. We tried to penetrate Jamaican life to the roots, but this book isn't meant to be encyclopedic. We didn't try to chronicle every important Jamaican musician. While we were on the island various reggae stars were touring abroad, and others were in hiding. Only Jah knows why. Some didn't want to be reached, and others we couldn't find. Reggae is in flux, constantly changing, a music that obstinately defies categorization. So rather than a history we present a portrait of reggae and Jamaica at what many feel is a turning point. And the cultural underpinnings of the reggae sensibility are unique and so tantalizing that even without the music we think they make a good story.

While we were in Jamaica the political climate shifted. A swift rise in politically parti-

san street violence literally shut down Kingston after dark. Outdoor dances were banned and the few nightclubs closed. The reggae musician had no place to play but the recording studio; the reggae listener had no music except the radio after midnight. The tensions were palpable as Jamaica struggled to cope with its fourteenth year of independence after three hundred years of the longest colonial administration in British history. And we saw the pressure almost imperceptibly changing the face of reggae music. Roots reggae has always been like a heartbeat, rhythmically stable and very restrained. But because Jamaica was tightening up one could see the musicians trying to produce a slicker, commercially viable sound that would expand the market for reggae even further. The chorus to a great reggae single, Marcia Griffith's "Survival," has become emblematic to all generations of Jamaicans, not just reggae musicians:

> *In times like these*
> *When survival is the game*
> *Let's play on*

2

Reggae Bloodlines

Jamaica: fragment of bomb-blast, catastrophe of geological history (volcano, middle passage, slavery, plantation, colony, neo-colony) has somehow miraculously—some say triumphantly—survived. How we did it is still a mystery and perhaps it should remain so. But at least we can say this: that the secret and expression of that survival lies glittering and vibrating in our music.

—*Edward Kamau Brathwaite*

From the beginning, Jamaica was never really a colonial settlement. From the middle of the seventeenth century the island was used more as a huge agricultural factory by a handful of British planters who reaped astronomical fortunes from sugar plantations worked by slaves imported from the Gold Coast of Africa. During the 250-year period that slavery was active in Jamaica some thirty million Africans were brought to the New World—the largest forced migration in human history. Among the thousands shipped to Jamaica were Ibos from lower Niger, Coromantee, Hausa, and Mandingo peoples from the Gold and Ivory Coasts, as well as people of the Noko, Yoruba, Sobo, and Nago nations. Jamaica's aboriginal Arawak Indians had almost all been killed by the Spaniards (who preceded the British) or had died from their diseases, leaving no mark upon their land but their

name for it—Xaymaca, Land of Springs.

The roots of reggae music are fixed in slavery. Slave orchestras were formed by several of the richer planters and entertained at such slave holidays as End of Crop Time, Piccaninny Christmas, Recreation Time, and the Grandee Balls. Rhythms, songs, and dances that are purely African have survived in rural Jamaica well into the twentieth century. A 1924 study of possible survivals of African song in Jamaica identifies African-derived work songs and grave songs in Western Jamaica's Cockpit Country as featuring part singing, antiphonal call-response chanting, and the repetition of single short musical phrases—all of which are characteristic of reggae. Among the Cockpit Maroon tribes—descendants of runaway slaves who fought the British to a draw a hundred years before Jamaican abolition and treatied themselves into an autonomous nation that still exists—the researchers of the 1924 study collected songs (called Coromantee songs by the Maroons) that speak of venerable African story figures —Anansi the spider and Jesta the trickster. Christmas time in Jamaica today is still celebrated by companies of John Canoe (or Junkanoo) dancers dressed in flashy rags, feathered headdresses, and black masks with features outlined in ghastly white. The dancers parade through the country towns, shouting and juking to African polyrhythm and the piping of the cane flutes. No one is sure what the John Canoe dance is all about save the obvious display of magic and spirit power, but the name has been traced to *dzong kunu,* "terrible sorcerer" in the West African Ewe tongue. With their music the slaves brought their spirits and fetishes. The *cumina* dance is still practiced throughout the island as a curative; black and white magic is practiced by *obeah* men and "science ladies" (Is your neighbor old Rupert killing your chocho vines with his cross-eyed stare? Have Mother Billeh fix up a powder and drop it into his ganja tea and either his eyes uncross or him drop dead. And then you have to go back to Mother Billeh to conquer Rupert's *duppy*—his ghost that's crawling into bed with you every night and wilting the bananas . . .). The various Afro-Caribbean fundamentalist cults that sprang up in Jamaica are also African in origin, especially the Pocomania ("Little Madness") churches that survive in Kingston and Montego Bay with their stark polytheism, syncopated drumming, and shuffling, breathy Pocomaniac trance: *wuh*-huh, *wuh*-huh, *wuh*-huh, *wuh*-huh, *wuh*-huh, *wuh*-huh . . .

Slavery was finally abolished in Jamaica in 1838, but the institution left a mark on the Jamaican descendants of African slaves that forms what ideological base reggae has. One of Jamaica's most popular reggae groups, Burning Spear, has a stinging, mesmerizing chant that is both rhetorical question and finger-pointing admonition: *Do you remember*

Junkanoo dancers

Pocomaniacs

the days of slavery? Do you remember the days of slavery? And in "Slave Driver," one of the Wailers' early numbers, Bob Marley eerily re-creates the anguish of a human chattel to the scratch of a harrowing reggae guitar chop:

> When I remember the crack of the
>   whip
> My blood runs cold
> I remember on the slave ship
> When they brutalized my very
>   soul.

Reggae is Jamaican soul music, a sort of tropic rock and roll with accents on the second and fourth beats, a metric system so flamboyant and unique that only seasoned Jamaican drummers can keep it together and flowing. Reggae has been around for years now, but many of the finest rock and jazz drummers in the world have been unable to master reggae time, and not for lack of trying.

Until the early Fifties, Jamaican music consisted only of *mento,* a depoliticized relation of the riotous calypso of Trinidad. Mento is also Jamaican adaptations of old British folk songs and sea chanteys. But where calypso is an exact science, a sophisticated vehicle for social comment, mento was often crude and dirty, so lewd, in fact, that the church in Jamaica kept some of the best mento recordings from being sold except under the counter. Jamaicans were content with mento until the early Fifties, when the island began to industrialize and change from an agro-oriented culture to an increasingly urbanized society. Kingston and the larger towns began to fill up,

King Tubby

and a new Jamaican—the bauxite worker, the factory hand, the longshoreman—left the rural parishes for the opportunities of the city. Today, twenty years later, some twenty thousand Jamaicans (out of a steady population of two million) still migrate to Kingston every year.

Right behind industrialization comes the awesome force of the transistor radio, but modern Jamaicans had been carefully monitoring Rhythm and Blues broadcasts from the States, most notably the AM stations roaring out of Miami and New Orleans when the nights were clear and the prevailing winds just right to float the sounds of Fats Domino, Amos Milburn, and the Louis Jordan bands right in for a landing in Jamaica, where the music was scrutinized, analyzed, taken apart, translated, assimilated, joked about, and put together

again. New Orleans R&B literally came off the boat; the Crescent City was and is the major port of export of things American to Kingston. But when it arrived, R&B was usually speeded up by local musicians who grew up with the slightly scattered pace of mento. As time progressed American R&B and soul music became the predominant music of the Caribbean, and in Jamaica particularly rapt attention was paid to anything new by Otis Redding, Sam Cooke (whose gospel voicings Jamaicans identified specially with), James Brown, Solomon Burke, Ben E. King, Chris Kenner, Lee Dorsey, and Brook Benton, who Bob Marley names as one of his principal favorites.

With the rise of R&B in Jamaica came the legendary "sound systems." Jamaican radio is government-controlled and was then too conservative for the steady diet of black blues that ordinary Jamaicans wanted to hear. Good R&B records were hard to come by and too expensive for most Jamaicans even when they were available, so a new entrepreneur entered the scene: the "sound-system man." More often than not, the sound systems were extensions of record shops, whose owner borrowed a van and loaded it with the biggest speakers he could find, a couple of turntables, and a stack of new sides just off the plane from New Orleans or Miami, and set up in somebody's back yard or out in a country market on a Saturday night. In the early Sixties competition among the various traveling discos got really intense. Pioneers like Duke Reid, Sir Coxone Dodd, and Prince Buster (they and countless imitators and pretenders invariably assumed titles of royalty—King Tubby is the penultimate) would scratch out the label of a hot new record so the competition would take longer to pick up on the song. Sound systems had vociferous followings whose collective ardor in support of the favorite disc jockey would send the claques of La Scala back to the woodwork in shame. When systems like Coxone's and Prince Buster's would set up within hearing distance of each other in the early days, squads of police usually were called in to control the resultant punch-outs.

Around 1960 the major R&B and pop music movements in America fizzled and died. Nobody knows why. It just happened. In Jamaica the sound systems were dependent for their livelihood on instantly accessible hit records that people could dance to. That kind of music never stopped coming in from New Orleans, but arrived in sufficient quantity only to keep a couple of systems alive and growing musically. Jamaicans couldn't and didn't identify with songs like "Palisades Park."

The slump in American music led directly to the beginnings of reggae. Frustrated by the lack of music coming in from the States, the sound-system men were forced to turn to local Jamaican music. This may not seem like a big deal until one realizes that, when it achieved its independence from Britain in 1962, Jamaica inherited a depressed colonial mentality and a gigantic national inferiority complex right out of Frantz Fanon's theories and 250 years of slavery. To educated Jamaicans anything British, American, or Canadian was vastly superior to anything home-grown. [Self-contempt has proven the greatest and most psychically expensive barrier for the Third World to transcend, and Jamaica is the example of this rather than the exception.] So when the sound-system men had to turn to Jamaican musicians to churn out an electric dance music for the brothers and sisters to get down and skank to, they were turning against history and fortune. Sound-system men styled themselves record producers, rented a little time at some ridiculous tinny two-track studio in Kingston—maybe Randy's on the North Parade—and found some country boy just in from Blue Hole or Alligator Pond and starving in the streets like Ivan O. Martin or Jimmy Cliff or Desmond Dekker—some nascent rude boy who learned to sing in church or school and was hungry and wolfish enough to compose a song about it—and they made records. The music was vibrant and loping; the dancers at the sound systems made up a dance to it and called the dance *ska,* and in time that became the name for Jamaican R&B. Ska. Cheerful, riddled with funky brass sections, disorganized, almost random. Ska was mento, Stateside R&B, and Jamaicans coming to terms with electric guitars and amplification. The sound systems became even more popular, and to get a bigger boom outdoors the deejays discovered all they had to do to both satisfy and stun their audiences was to turn the bass knobs all the way up to the pain threshold. Today the bass-driven mojo of the best reggae is derived precisely from the needs of recorded music loud outdoors.

Ska music stayed in Kingston and the West

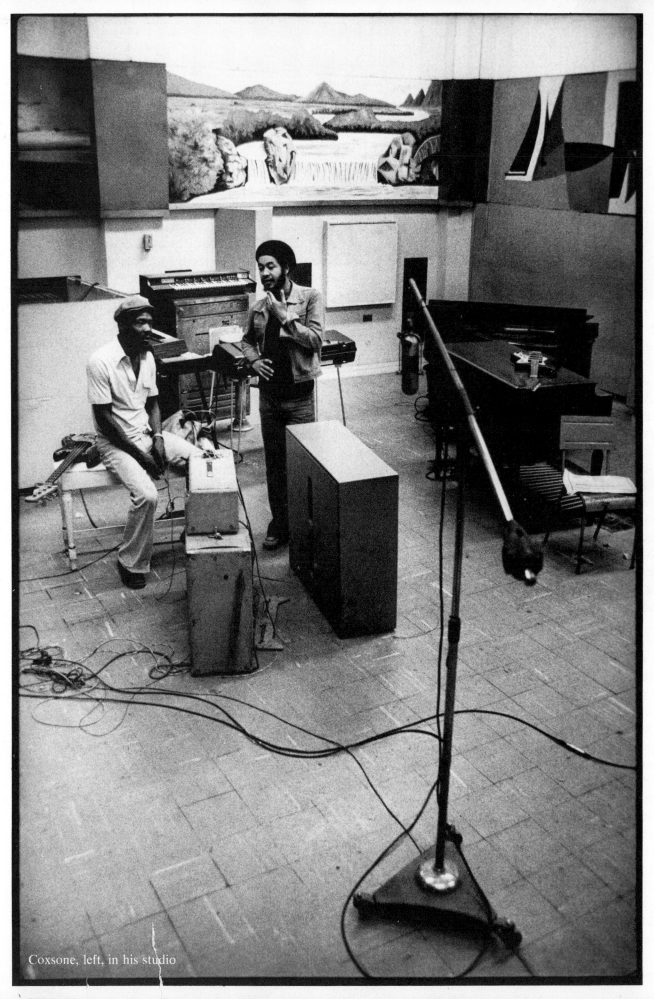

Coxsone, left, in his studio

Indian ghettos of East London until 1964, when a then fledgling white Jamaican producer named Chris Blackwell recorded a ska tune, "My Boy Lollipop," by a singer named Millie Small, and released it in England, where it was the first West Indian record to make number one on the British charts. The tune also did well in Europe and was a respectable hit in the States. Jamaican music had been presented to the world for the first time and seemed to have passed the test. Wrongfully anticipating a planetary ska craze after Small's hit, dozens of Jamaican musicians and British-based black bands had a go at ska singles. Some of the minor hits of the period were "Darling Patricia," by Owen Gray; "Miss Jamaica," by the fifteen-year-old Jimmy Cliff; "Rough and Tough," by the Strangers; "Housewives Choice," by Derrick Morgan; and "Jamaica Ska," by Byron Lee and the Ska Kings. Sound-system-man-turned-producer Prince Buster churned out forgettable but qualitatively good ska singles that kept the music barely respectable as it became more pallid and faceless with each modification.

No one can really identify the point at which the Jamaican dance music called ska evolved into and was ultimately replaced by a new dance called "rock-steady." The prevailing theory is that the bitterly hot and dry summer of 1966 retarded the bouncy tempo of the ska dancers and necessitated what one observer has called a "slow, painful, almost sinister" dance—rock-steady. By the mid-Sixties the sound-system men were devoting all their energy to recording singles, hustling them at home, promoting them in England, and as usual robbing the singers to their socks. Too busy to attend to their mobile discos, they hired disc jockeys to run them, and the best of these later would become major stars and cult figures in their own right. With the influx of British cash, the producers improved their techniques and equipment. Fewer instruments

were required to produce the basic rock-steady sound; rhythm and bass guitars, drums, and organ became the typical instrumental lineup. An occasional horn section might be thrown in to record. The music was called rock-steady very aptly; as a dance beat it was *steadier* and more dependable than the vagaries of ska. The sound was more substantial and carried more internal meaning than the airiness of the best of ska. Lyrical content exposed the consciousness of the artist for the first time. No longer were songs exclusively about love and making love, the preoccupations of ska; a rock-steady tune might deal with the police, hungry children, or even the disc jockey U Roy's astounding evocation of Dubček and the Russian invasion of Czechoslovakia in his version of "Listen to the Teacher." The big rock-steady hit outside of Jamaica was Max Romeo's lewd "Wet

Max Romeo

Dream" (second verse: "Look how you big and fat, like a big clot, give the crumpet to big foot Joe, give the fanny to me . . ."), which is said to have sold a million copies in England in 1967 without having gone on the charts. Max claimed later the song was about a leaky roof.

The dance that replaced rock-steady, around 1968, was called "reggae." Again, no one knows for certain where that word comes from. Some trace it to the Jamaican dialect word for raggedness. The word appears first on a 1967 dance record by the Maytals called "Do the Reggay." I once asked Toots Hibbert, lead singer of the Maytals and composer of "Do the Reggay," to tell me what the word meant, and his answer is as satisfactory a definition of reggae as you're likely to get: "Reggae means comin' from the people, y'know? Like a everyday thing. Like from the ghetto. From *majority*. Everyday thing that people use like food, we just put music to it and make a dance out of it. Reggae mean *regular* people who are suffering, and don't have what they want." The reggae sound was even slightly slower than rock-steady and much more powerful due to the emphasis of the bass as the principal melodic drive of most songs. Social, political, and spiritual concepts entered the lyrics more and more, until the reggae musicians became Jamaica's prophets, social commentators, and shamans.

In Jamaica in the late Sixties most of the younger, up-and-coming reggae performers sprang out of the "Rude Boy" phenomenon. Rudies were young men, aged anywhere between fourteen and thirty (most Jamaican youths leave school at fourteen if not earlier), who had joined the migration from country to Kingston. With no skills and Jamaica's chronic 35-per-cent unemployment rate, the Rudies redefined street life (hanging out, flicking deadly German ratchet knives, trolley-hopping, purse-snatching, occasional muggings, petty theft, rum, insolence, ganja, sing-

The Maytals, circa 1965

ing, and general hooliganism) into lifetime careers, most of which ended very early. For the Rudie the only way out of the gross tropical shantytowns of West Kingston (Trench Town, Tivoli Gardens, Ghost Town, Jones Town, Denham Town, Olympic Gardens) was via a hit single or a police bullet. The ethos of Rude Boy was pure punk—being the most relentless, outrageous, rudest, best-looking, baddest character on the gullybank. And the archetypal Rude Boy was the Slickers' "Johnnie Too Bad":

Walking down the road with a
    pistol in your waist
Johnny you're too bad
Walking down the road with a ratchet
    in your waist

Johnny you're too bad
You're jesta robbing and stabbing
   and looting and shooting
Y'know you're too bad
One of these days when you hear a
   voice say come
Where you gonna run to?
You gonna run to the rock for rescue
There will be no rock

What is the rock the Slickers refer to in "Johnny Too Bad"? The rock of the Church? Rude Boy concerns are also spelled out in Desmond Dekker's "Shanty Town":

And now rude boys have a wail
Cause dem out a jail
Rude Boys cannot fail
Cause dem must get bail
Dem a loot, dem a shoot, dem a wail
A shanty town

The Rudies knew the truths of *The Harder They Come* long before the film was made. The Rude Boy countered his lack of discipline with attention to thought-force, the idea that Jimmy Cliff articulates when he sings "You Can Get It if You Really Want." The Rude Boys, in the heart of their cocky, ragged despair, *knew* that Cliff and Dekker and the rest were just like them, and most Rudies thought if they could just get into Leslie Kong's studio long enough to wail their song they could show they could outsing, outrave, outsmoke and outlove any of them. Many Rudies died young. Some grew up. Others grew dreadlocks and claimed they were Rastamen all along.

In Jamaica from the beginning reggae was slum music and was disdained by all but the lowest classes of black society. Its mento and Rude Boy origins gave it a crude and antisocial air with the beaten threat of violence projected by the Rudies. When reggae music arrived in England it wasn't even taken that seriously. British disc jockeys openly ridiculed reggae, and new songs from Jamaica were sometimes played contemptuously by programmers trying to remain open to new sounds. Ironically it was to the violence-prone British youth cult of Skinhead that lilting reggae most appealed in England. The Skinheads, when they weren't bashing Pakistani immigrants or wantonly demolishing railroad trains after soccer games, were usually to be found in any of the many reggae discos that went aboveground in London in 1968. If reggae was ever in the slightest danger of gaining respectability upon reaching the British Isles, the leering specter of Skinhead, the U.K. variant of Rude Boy, solved that problem once and for all.

Reggae hit the British Isles hard long before it was even heard with regularity in the States, primarily because of the massive migration from the West Indies to England in the postwar years. Today there are full-fledged reggae bands in England (although the music is patently slicker and more commercial, composed of Jamaicans who have never set foot on Jamaica. Reggae outfits like Greyhound and The Cimarrons are at the head of the British-based West Indian bands who have capitalized on reggae's success with whites.

The last great wellspring of reggae is Rastafarian music. The Rastafarians are members of Jamaica's spiritual nationality—millenarian in outlook, esoteric and fundamentalist in origin, Back-to-Africa/Redemptionist in temperament, worshipers of Haile Selassie as the living God, the predominant cultural force in Jamaica for the past thirty years. Their contribution to reggae is seminal. The basic Rasta rhythm is a sustained two-beat riff that swells and hypnotizes like a heartbeat. (An example is the Wailers' version of "Rastaman Chant.") Rastafarian drumming stems from one of the older Jamaican musical forms, *burra,* now practiced almost exclusively in Trench Town and other West Kingston areas. Burra uses three large double-membrane drums usually made of rum kegs and goatskin. The largest is the bass drum; the repeater and the funde are

3

A Visit with the Black Prince of Reggae

Jamaica, land of wood and water
Motor vehical and man-slaughter

Dillinger, *"No Chuck It"*

Them belly full but we hungry
A hungry man is an angry man
A hungry mob is an angry mob
A rain a fall but the dutty tough
A pot a cook but the food no 'nough
You're gonna dance to Jah music—dance
We're gonna dance to Jah music—dance
Forget your troubles and dance
Forget your sorrows and dance
Forget your sickness and dance
Forget your weakness and dance

Bob Marley, *"Them Belly Full"*

You scream into Jamaica over an aquamarine Caribbean mirror in a jet, nonstop to Montego Bay. In search of reggae music, you're a little annoyed that Air Jamaica doesn't program reggae on its in-flight recordings. Your uneasiness is confirmed a few minutes after you step out of the pressurized jet into the afternoon burn of the tropics, the sky so clear and bright that you're momentarily blinded by the diamonds of sunshine glistening

off the water nearby. You step into the customs shed and pass the stoned and broken calypso/mento quartet that greets every plane in straw hats, bare feet, and aloha-barf shirts, musicians so red-eyed and haggered that it looks like Judge Dread sentenced them to play for tourists rather than do time for ganja trading. You try not to listen as you pass them, but the hoarse, hopeless scratching gets to you anyway.

The customs agent opens your metal case and checks out your tape recorder, and asks if you are a musician coming down for the reggae. You say yes, just to get it over with, and he peruses your new issues of *Black Music,* which won't be on sale in Jamaica for another month. He checks it carefully and then motions you into the customs office. You wonder if you're going to get shaken down, but instead he turns up the radio because it's playing "Marcus Garvey," by Burning Spear. The agent tells you Spear is the best band in Jamaica, better even than the Wailers, and to be sure to get their records. You say you'll do your best.

You lease a Datsun from the Chinese woman at the airport and nearly kill yourself and your photographer when you forget to drive on the left as you pull onto the highway. A truckload of shirtless youths misses you by inches, your photographer shrieks, you swerve

to the left, and the youths speed away laughing and cursing you. *Bumba clot Yankee!* It's too late in the day to make Kingston, a hundred miles and five hours of two-lane coastal and mountain roads away. So you hole up for the night in an old MoBay hotel called the Chatham Beach, reminiscent of colonial days with its tiled verandas and starched, smiling young waiters. You take a swim, walk on the beach, get the pulse of the island into your head. Dinner is good flounder and boiled chocho, many bottles of Red Stripe beer, and another, slightly more presentable calypso band which does an awful version of the naughty reggae ditty "Shaving Cream." The tourist spots on the North Coast still think calypso is the national music. It's a nice hotel, but the place is full of geeks and you want to get out. In your room you listen to the radio. The political wars in Kingston are getting worse, the Minister of Finance has just announced an $81 million tax hike and new import restrictions in an attempt to save the island's teetering economy; the airwaves are full of irate Jamaicans calling the late night talk shows and complaining about taxes and inflation in Carib patois. It's past midnight and they should be playing reggae, but you flick around the dial and all you get is talk show *labberish*

Cane truck

and Radio Havana's broadcast of Fidel's latest four-hour tirade.

In the morning you hit the road for Kingston and remember to drive on the left. At the first gas station the attendant tells you not to go to Kingston because it's too dangerous. You tell him you're going anyway and he suggests you might want to smoke a little something for the ride. But you've heard about roadblocks and you politely refuse. On the road you notice that everyone is driving as fast as possible, passing slow cane trucks on uphill curves at 85 mph, taunting and hopefully beating death. The road is strewn with burned

Along the North Coast

car hulks every few miles, grim reminders of chances taken and missed. You drive through Falmouth, where Marcus Garvey preached, and it looks to you like an African town. You point east along the coast and skirt Discovery Bay, where Columbus anchored when he discovered Jamaica; Runaway Bay, where the last of the Spaniards abandoned the island to the pirates and the British; and St. Ann's Bay, where Garvey was born. The coast road is so green with sugar cane and palm and the sun so yellow that when the two meet the whole world seems to turn *blue*. You share the road with cattle and goats and peasants walking along, their machetes gently slapping the sides of their legs. Everywhere billboards advertise Panther condoms. One of the planet's erogenous zones.

Just before you turn south at Ocho Rios, you come across a bauxite plant and the air gets red and dusty. Bauxite, the raw material for aluminum, is Jamaica's major source of foreign currency, and everywhere you go you'll see bloody red gashes carved out of deep green mountains. You'll hear that Jamaica is literally selling itself to stay alive. At Ocho Rios you turn right into Fern Gully, a steep canyon incline that follows the bed of one of the old rivers. A road crew is working up above, but there are no flags up. You ignore or don't really hear a cry of warning and a two-ton piece of canyon wall smashes in front of your skidding car. Speeding cars and motorcycles scream to a stop behind you, the photographer cowers under the seat, your nerves are prickly and you wish you'd taken

up the gasoline attendant on that spliff he offered you. You climb through dark Fern Gully and emerge into the Blue Mountains, twisting along the bad road through tiny hamlets in a perfect lush landscape. Through Mango Alley and Mount Rosser, by the big red Alcan plant at Ewarton, through Linstead and Bog Walk, over the flat bridge at Raby's Corner. In two hours, you're near Spanish Town, on the outskirts of Kingston, and the faraway smell of something burning tickles your nose and your eyes.

And you enter the City of Fires. The air is harsh with the sweet scent of burning cane and bonfires. The outskirts of Kingston are shantytowns, and as you speed down Washington Boulevard you think you might have gotten on the wrong plane and wound up in Senegal. The roadside is riotous with human and animal life, and it feels somehow good and comforting to be part of it. As you stream with the traffic down Half Way Tree in the middle of town, the smell of fire intensifies. The sun shines hard through the ashen haze, and you learn why fire and burning are the prime metaphors of roots reggae.

You check into your hotel, a small block building full of diplomats and eccentric expatriates in residential New Kingston. It has a pool and palms and a little restaurant and is inexpensive, and you think you're doing well. After you unpack you walk around the place, and a young red-jacketed porter of East Indian descent checks you out and asks if you need anything to smoke. A hour later he reappears with a paper poke full of leafy ganja

ingston

In Trench Town

buds, all you can smoke in two weeks for a dollar.

Again it's late in the day, so you make some calls, run a few errands, sit on your little patio with a Red Stripe, and watch the lights winking through the dusk from affluent homes in the mountains overlooking the city. You turn to the radio and they're alternating an occasional reggae track with Miami disco music. Later, long after dinner, the place is shutting down for the night and you walk outside to get the fresh air blowing in off the harbor. The pool is dark and quiet; the only sounds come from the street at the end of the hotel's long driveway. And there's not even much traffic. Citizens, even in New Kingston, have stopped traveling on the streets at night since January 1976, when political violence against the government increased in a raging crime wave. It

was said that even the Kingston police stayed out of sight at night if they could.

Now you hear a rustling in the bushes next to your patio and you get the rush of adrenalin that says, *This is it*. But it's only an old man, about seventy, who moves his chair out of the bush where he's been resting. He tells you he's the night watchman, and the two of you share a cigarette. You listen to the reassuring patter of the old village wiseman: "Sure, t'ings happen . . . and t'ings pass . . . Bettah soon come . . ." The old man has the terrifying job of protecting the property from marauding thugs who migrate nightly from the slums to New Kingston. The old watchman is by himself, with no access to weapons or even a telephone, since everything is locked. His only armament is a bipitched constable's whistle which he blows should a quintet of Rude Boys slink into the parking lot and start jacking up a big Mercedes for the tires.

Late that night you're woken out of a light sleep by the watchman's whistle and scuffling sounds outside. From the fragile white-haired old man comes the disguised deep baritone of a husky thirty-year-old cane cutter. "What a-guan on out deh? Derek! Derek! Call the *police!*" He sounds his shrill whistle again and starts to clank the lawn furniture around and make a general commotion that wakes everyone in the place. There is, of course, no Derek. After a superb ten-minute performance and much warlike blustering, whatever had disturbed the old man has retreated, and he sits back down in the shadows. Only the red coal at the end of his cigarette is visible. Jah only knows what would happen if the Rudies ever took the trouble one night to call the watchman's bluff.

In Jamaica things happen at a tropical pace, even in Kingston, and in the morning you find it's going to take a while to make contact and set up appointments. For the most part the master musicians of reggae don't have phones, and you learn it's going to be tricky, this searching for reggae music, and that you're going to have to depend on your luck. So you decide to take a drive through Trench Town. You have been warned not to do it, that Trench Town is too gross and dangerous for outsiders, and that these are bad days even to be in Jamaica. But you've spent too many hours listening to "Trench Town Rock" to be able to tell yourself you know what reggae's all about without having seen its Mecca.

Once, western Kingston was a little fishing village, quiet and even picturesque. But thirty years ago the government decided to fill part of the harbor, and what they used was Kingston's garbage. As the landfill took shape it was occupied by landless squatters from the hills. For housing they used a few pieces of scrap wood and rusty corrugated tin under which whole families existed without water or electricity. The shantytowns—Trench Town, Ghost Town, the Dungle—grew up literally on a dump of trash and human waste. A limbo of flies and misery and child death comparable to the worst of Calcutta. A moonscape of degradation that birthed some of the wildest social and cultural phenomena of this century —the Rastafarians, the Rude Boys, and reggae. A squalid place to sit around doing nothing, waiting for the pressure to drop.

So you drive down Slipe Road, stopping at a stand to get a sack of spicy goat patties for breakfast. When you reach the city square known as the Parade, you turn right onto Marcus Garvey Drive, then right again to Central Road and you're in the thick of it. But no one bothers you and things seem cool enough to roll down the windows. You're caught off-guard by all the greenery and the palm trees that shade the ramshackle huts and houses. Children and dogs dart in front of your car. The sun is bright, and people look as they do everywhere else. You realize about Trench Town that half of what they say is true and the rest is hyperbole.

But it's a long way from Trench Town behind Bob Marley's mansion/commune on Hope Road, where the Black Prince of Reggae is languoring on the hood of his silver BMW Bavaria under a poinciana tree, working hard on an eight-inch spliff. Every third or fourth draw Marley puffs up a cumulonimbus of smoke and momentarily disappears like a genie being sucked back into his lamp. Every time he apotheosizes into a cloud like that you wonder where he goes for that brief interval before the fog lifts and he reappears before you, waiting politely for your next question. . . .

From the reggae cottage industry of sound systems, two-track studios, and sharp hustlers emerged a triumvirate of major artists and musical groupings: Jimmy Cliff, Toots and the Maytals, and Bob Marley and the Wailers.

Among reggae musicians Cliff is respected and the Maytals venerated, but Marley and the Wailers are recognized as the king cats, the number-one dread roots of the music; Marley is seen as the pathfinder for the rest of the reggae desperadoes out into the frontiers of Middle America, Europe, and even back to Africa where reggae records are now said to sell as well as James Brown's.

In Jamaica now they call Robert Nesta Marley the Negus of reggae music; meaning the semidivine Ultimate. But this kind of adulation comes hard and seldom, and it is only after fifteen years of scuffling and wearying poverty that Marley and the Wailers are getting their shot at being culture heroes beyond the shores of Jamaica.

Bob Marley was born in 1945 in St. Ann, the garden parish, at a spot called Rhoden Hall, so small it's not on the map. His mother was a local woman, his father a major retired from the British Army and having a go at the life of a colonial. Marley says he's only seen his father once or twice, nothing unusual in Jamaica, where colonial mores are a thing of the past and people tend to be raised by their mothers. Marley went to school in St. Ann; when he was fourteen he left the rural parish and headed for Kingston. When asked what he did next Marley laughs, takes another draw, and says he moved to Trench Town and became a welder. But you don't know if he's serious because he's laughing and "welding" is the standard reply of many Rasta musicians

Peter Tosh

Marley wasn't the only writer among the Wailers. His obsession with the cruelties of slavery was shared by Peter Tosh, who wrote the brimstone text of "400 Years" as well as "Stand Up for Your Rights," which in time would become the Wailers' clarion call. Asked to pose for pictures for their British record company in 1970, the Wailers were posed and snapped skulking around a suburban yard in Black Power berets, clutching toy submachine guns and automatic pistols.

The Wailers in their prime were the best of the part-singing reggae vocal trios. Marley's

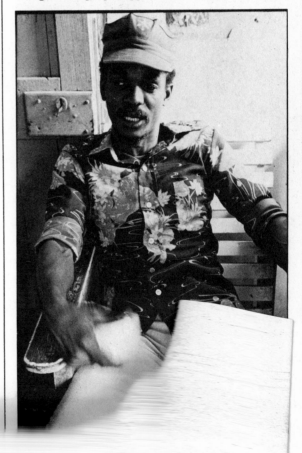

playing chicken-scratch rhythm guitar, Tosh playing lead guitar, and Bunny Livingston harmonizing and playing hand drums. With producer Lee Perry the Wailers recorded what many think are their best songs, and Bob Marley began to receive attention as a lyricist of imposing passion and dark power. Marley's trademark was setting incantatory, defiantly rebellious words to the sweetest and most lilt-ing of melodies. Thus the old Wailers' loveliest song, "Trench Town Rock," celebrated a bru-tal 1967 street riot in Kingston. A favorite Marley lyric preoccupation was hu

Aston "Family Man" Barrett

(Neville Livingston) Bunny Wailer

tative in both tone and style. They were the first of the really strong Jamaican groups to adopt the abstemious, continually testifying life of the Rastafarian, incorporating elements of Rasta drumming into their music long before it became fashionable for reggae groups to do so.

After recording with Lee Perry, the Wailers came upon another of the fallow periods that plagued their career. Marley, who like most reggae masters would sign anything for a couple of hundred dollars in those days, signed a songwriting and publishing contract with Johnny Nash, who had picked up on reggae as the vehicle for his creative rebirth. Nash actually took Marley to Sweden for a few months to work on song projects (what the winter-hating Marley, who once canceled a Wailers tour of England because it snowed, thought of

Sweden is unfortunately unknown). Nash later recorded and made moderate hits of Marley's sexy "Guava Jelly" and "Stir It Up." Ironically Nash would be the first international popularizer of reggae when he recorded "I Can See Clearly Now," a worldwide hit in 1971.

In 1972 the Wailers got their ticket to commercial success in Babylon when they were signed to a recording contract by Chris Blackwell, the scion of a wealthy Jamaican planting family who had parlayed a love of his native music into a successful small independent record label, Island Records. Blackwell's strategy was to promote the Wailers' natural genius into the newest and potentially hardest-rocking musical force in the world. After meeting with the Wailers in London, Blackwell gave them the money to go back to Kingston, hire a

Bob Marley and I-Threes
(Rita Marley, Judy Mowatt, Marcia Griffiths)

I-Threes

could now stay away from the grim jazz rooms and play large halls. Marley, his locks fully grown and spread like the mane of the Lion of Judah, had become *the* reggae shaman, a weaver of strands of thin air and Rasta vibrations into a harmonious pattern of rugged morality, fearless protest, and transcendent music.

The sign on the gate of the big pink house on Hope Road says "Island House"; it was headquarters for Chris Blackwell's Jamaican operation until he gave the place to Marley. Now, while the corrugated tin roof is under repair and the interior is being rebuilt and

Island House

The House of Dread—Alan "Skilly" Cole, bottom cent[er]

"Yeah, mon! Rasta mon must go home to Africa. It sound funny to some people sometime. Sometime sounds like a mad thing. But it is our real desire fe go home to Africa. Certain things that happen a long time ago must be revealed, and until that happen . . . I and I still in captivity."

Would Rastafarians settle for making Jamaica like Africa?

"No! No settle for Jamaica. We like Jamaica, y'know. But Jamaica is spoiled as far as Rastaman is concerned. The history of Jamaica is spoiled, just like if ya have an egg that break ya kyaan put it back together again. Jamaica kyaan be fixed for I and I, for Rastaman. When we check out the system here we see death. And Rastaman seh, Life! Here people must fight for everything."

Reggae musicians have been scolded here in Jamaica for selling Jamaican culture. . . .

Stevie Wonder and Bob Marley at National
Stadium, Kingston, November 1975

"It is not selling our culture. If God hadn't
given me a song to sing I wouldn't have a song
to sing. Look: 'Until the philosophy which
holds one race superior and another inferior is
finally and permanently discredited and abandoned, there is war . . .' God [Haile Selassie]
say dem things. Me check them out to the people. Ya kyaan sell culture."

Are you going to Africa someday?

"Yeah, mon! Time is now, y'know what I
mean? Is plenty of I and I. Marcus Garvey
seh: 'Africa towards Africans.' Ya kyaan argue
with that.

"All that is causin' the problem is devil
needin' everybody's life. But here ya kyaan
work for what ya want. Ya can never reach
the goal. The system kill people so we must
kill the system. Every mon want fe drive car,
nobody wants to ride donkey.

"Only one government me love, the government of Rastafari. We come from Africa and
none of the leaders want fe accept it. They
want us fe think we are all Jamaicans. The
majority of people in Jamaica want fe go
home to Africa, but the leaders say you must
stay and die here. Today is not the day, but
when it happen 144,000 of us go home. We
talkin' about the twelve tribes of Israel.

Twelve tribes! Government wrong. With the
government, I don't know what a-guan on.
Politicians don't care fe people, only Jah care.
Seh, every man for himself, and God for us
all. [Marley passes over the spliff. Things turn
to haze. Motorbikes roar in and out of the
yard.] Yeah, mon! This is war! Jamaica is
hell, y'know. Until we find our roots again
politics will still be a thing. If we find the roots
again, we can *live*.

"Reggae music, soul music, rock music—
every song is a sign. But ya have fe be careful
of the type of song and vibration that ya give
fe the people, for 'woe be unto they who lead
my people astray.' As a singer I personally
like to sing for the people rather than sing for
half the people. Ya have fe be careful of the
song you sing. And if Babylon come fe exploit
us, it just make Babylon fall faster. If we are
true brothers money is not a separation for us.
Y'understand? Good.

"Yes, people rob me and try fe trick me, but
now I have experience. Now I know and I see

when people don't hear it on the radio them have it in the house, and go dance and hear it. Radio is important but once song come out and you don't hear it on radio, the big promotion is that the song is banned, and when song is banned everyone want fe hear it. Hyuh hyuh hyuh . . .

"Don't talk to me of Manley and government. Manley don't know what a-guan on, mon. Manley kyaan stop prophecy. Prophecy has to have its course. The herb is the healing of the nations. Manley can say whatever [about legalizing ganja], but police get their orders from somebody. Manley come here one time and smoke. No, I and I brethren smoke. Me and Manley never smoke together yet, hyeeuh!

"I don't condemn people. I leave all judgment to Jah. We don't condemn the individual, we condemn the system. There are those who live in evil and think it is right. For instance now, a Rastaman sit down and smoke some herb, with good meditation, and a policeman come see him, stick him up, search him, beat him, and put him in prison. Now, *who is this guy doing these things for?* Herb grow like yams and cabbage. Just *grow*. Policeman do these things fe evil.

"Rasta seh, it is good to think good of yourself and others. Inspiration come straight out of Jah, mon. Yeah, mon. *Yeah, mon.* The ship rock, but we still steady.

"Rum mosh up your insides. Just kill ya, like the system. System don't agree with herb because herb make ya too solid. Y'see, when ya smoke herb ya conscience come right in front of ya. Ya *see* it. Y'see? So the devil, he no like it if ya stay conscious and clean up your life. For devil see ya not guan fe do fool thing again. Yes, Rasta! Herb is the healing of the nation.

"Many more will have fe suffer, many more will have fe die, no ask me why. But Rasta not violent. Rasta *physical*. Y'know what I mean? We no come like them sheep in them slaughter, y'know what I mean? Them just don't

and I don't get tricked. Used to make recordings and not get royalties. Still happen sometime. All Wailers records made here, but them pirated to England. All of them English companies *rob,* mon. Everybody that deals with West Indian music . . . *thieves."*

What reggae musicians do you respect?

"I-Threes. Burning Spear. Big Youth. All Jamaican music. Me love dub [instrumental reggae], but I don't get involved with it too much. Dub means right and tight, the perfect groove. When Wailers seh *dub* this one, dis mean we gonna play it right and tight."

Why don't you hear much reggae on the radio in Jamaica?

"It's because the music shows the real situation in Jamaica. Some people don't like to hear the real truth. But it doesn't matter:

have power to do certain things to I and I."

Do you ever fear for your own safety because of the political situation?

"No, sir. No, mon. I not afraid fe them. If I can avoid them I avoid them. If I'm going down the street and I see a roadblock and there's a street for me fe turn off before the roadblock I better go and turn off. Is a *blood clot,* anyway. If somebody want kill me, if somebody want fe try hurt I, and if the only thing I can do is defend Iself, I'm the one. Yes, mon. *I'm the one, and let no one on it.*

"Gun Court? A wickedness, mon."

Other Rastas have criticized you for selling yourself to Babylon and point to your car as an example of your materialism. . . .

"Well, BMW not the system. Babylon the system. [He spits and kisses his teeth contemptuously.] Some say BMW mean Bob Marley and Wailers. BMW mean . . . British Made War car or something like that. This car

doesn't belong to me. This car belong to the *road.* That who the car belong to. Better than donkey. It don't feed all night and mosh up the bush and in the morning it don't bray and make noise. *Hyuh hyuh hyuh hyuh hyuh.* [He takes a swooping draw on his spliff—*Ssswwffffftt!*] I and I prefer goat to donkey. If ya see a goat ya supposed fe start communicating with the goat. A goat smart, y'know. When ya lick a goat with ya car ya sad. Yes, Rasta! Any man ram a goat is sad. Better drive careful and don't gamble."

Do you have a prediction for your future and reggae?

"I and I and I reason, ya watch what a-guan happen. It not take long. I kyaan explain it because if me have the power fe explain it, I explain it and people will try fe stop me. Me know it gonna happen. But reggae going to get a real fight; it happen already. This is Third World music. Ya don't have understanding in one day. Ya have it little by little, and ya just know. It grow.

It was past twilight in Marley's yard, and over the horizon the sliver of waxing moon shone like a street lamp. As we conversed, dark figures gathered in the shadows around the car, listening intently as Marley spoke. A young beauty pressed in, concentrating on Marley's discourse with the foreigner. After a while the shaman finished his spliff and lapsed into the realms of ganja-land.

The master spaced out and a young Rasta brother took over with a lecture on the twelve tribes of Israel and challenged the visitor on his negligible knowledge of biblical lore. The boy arrogantly demanded to know how long it takes to read the Bible a chapter a day, and when the visitor said he didn't know the youth snorted that it took three and a half years. The visitor said that for some people it was a big decision to come back to the Bible, and the Rasta pointed out with irritation that all it took was your ears. Marley woke up and agreed: "Read the Bible, mon. Most populous book in the world. Certain things ya have fe know what fe do, ya read the Bible." Then he spaced out again. Another old Dread handed the visitor a spliff and asked for some money, but Marley came to and told him to lay off. As the visitor said his thanks and farewells, he was followed out of the yard by the Bible-belting youth, who was offering for sale a brown paper poke of ganja. The visitor turned around and his last image of the Black Prince of Reggae was of Marley sleeping on the hood of his car, surrounded by his disciples, who seemed to be affectionately watching his slumber.

Kingston is a small city, everyone seems to know everyone else, and Bob Marley is in a delicate position. Every move he makes is watched with intense interest. The contra-

→ 27A   → 28   →

dictions inherent in the commercialization of reggae are acute. Proponents of pure roots reggae maintain that the Wailers' sophistication and success will ultimately dilute the music's energy. Marley's defenders point out that reggae has always had a commercial right wing and a roots left wing, and that so far the Wailers remain one of the most powerful electric bands in the world while staying ideologically on the left.

But they're saying that Marley is finding himself under heavy political pressure these days. Jamaican politicians have always used reggae songs and musicians in their campaigns; Marley has been approached by both sides in Jamaica's smoldering civil strife. Jamaican politics can get extremely rough, and Marley has been heard to complain that the politicians were leaning on him and he felt he might have to leave the country for a while. The Black Prince of Reggae in contemplation of exile must be a very troubled man.

The Wailers in Los Angeles,
Don Taylor at the wheel

Burning Spear at Chela Bay

4

Burning Spear at Chela Bay

Young people from all over North America and Europe are flying into Jamaica expecting to be immersed in reggae, expecting to drown in music. Instead they drown in the realities of the Third World. Yes, Jamaican cities and towns pump along to the sound of reggae blasting from the tinny speakers of record shops, and when you can find a dance or a sound system, you'll see people performing the swaying motions—stepping lightly in place to the beat, arms swaying and churning as if in a stationary walking race. But reggae is a recorded music, not a performing one. Reggae's origins were to fill the needs of the sound systems, not to fill dance halls and nightclubs with live musicians. Most reggae recordings are played by a handful of studio groups in Kingston, and on the whole island there are probably less than a dozen bands capable of handling the strength and subtlety that a live reggae performance requires. Visitors to Jamaica usually get their reggae from the same sources as Jamaicans—from the radio and jukeboxes, sound systems and record stores. For the reggae musician, that means he either plays in the studios or rehearses in back yards or local churches, depending on whether he can hustle equipment, amplifiers, and electricity.

The only reggae club in Jamaica, the one place on the whole island that books the top reggae musicians, is owned and operated by young Americans. The name of the club is Roots, and it is in the basement of the Chela Bay Hotel, outside of Ocho Rios on the North Coast. A few days after our arrival in Kingston an advertisement appeared in the *Daily Gleaner* announcing that one of the best reggae groups in the world, Burning Spear, would play the club that weekend.

Kingston is like any big town. On the weekends those who can get away head for the mountains or the beach, usually somewhere on

49

tains. For a few cents we buy baked ears of corn and roasted breadfruit eaten with slivers of salt fish, long strings of tangerines and oranges, bananas right off the tree, massive pineapples, and thin-skinned, deep red and blushingly juicy pears called Ethiopian apples, whose delicate taste causes the eyes to roll way back into the head with ecstasy.

We pick up a load of fruit for later and get back on the road. The gray sky opens and it pours for an hour. When we hit the top of Fern Gully, we launch into a slithering two-mile skid down the slick forest road, emerging narrowly with our lives. Chela Bay is ten miles farther east along the coast road, in the hamlet of Boscobel.

The only reggae club in Jamaica turned out to be in the dungeon of an old colonial relic,

Roots Bunnies at the Playboy Club

the lush North Coast, and the roads, treacherous and steep even when empty, are full on a Saturday morning. Overloaded cane trucks belch up the mountain roads at a snail's crawl, spewing inky black soot into the lungs of the hapless drivers behind. The only way to survive is roll up the windows and pass on a hairpin turn with a Mercedes blasting its horn hysterically as it hurtles straight at us, offering no quarter at seventy downhill as we struggle past the cane truck at forty. Pure suicide. After a couple hours of this we're only halfway to Ocho. We pass a large river the color of red clay and carrot juice, and someone mutters that the river is a dump for bauxite waste. Soon we come to a hillside cluster of evil-looking shanties which turn out to be fruit stands, offering for sale the bounty of the Blue Moun-

the sort of large white multitiered villa to be found on the Italian Riviera, sprawling at the end of a sparkling white sand beach. When the place was built forty or so years ago, it must have been quietly comfortable and very beautiful. But ten years ago a Playboy Club Hotel was erected next door, running the entire length of the little beach, a scabrous and skeletal building that destroyed the area's tranquillity. Jamaican women were turned into Bunnies and fitted with uplift swimsuit brassieres. They bobbled sexlessly around the beach bringing rum punches to lobster-hued French-Canadians. The clientele of the two hotels—the Canuck playboys and the shaggy white hipoisie and wasted-looking Dreadlocks who hung around the Chela Bay—shared the beach and eyed each warily.

Clarence and Alaric were two Dreadlocks

who said they were on their way to Negril, but they might be going back to Kingston too. Rastafarians don't believe in time, death, processed food, or the demise of Haile Selassie, so it's sometimes hard to get specifics from them. They were temporarily squatting in a bare little room the hotel's management courteously made available to visiting musicians and Rastafarian brethren, and were nourishing themselves on a dusty green hillock of ganja pollen. There was about a pound of these furry, tiny cannabis leaves (known in Morocco as *kif*) wrapped in a dozen generations of old newsprint and Manila hemp paper. Clarence was wrapped in an orange cape decorated with rampant lions, and kept dipping his bamboo pipe into the kif. He had been fasting and meditating for days on the road and was feeling very exalted. A dip of the pipe, a match, a long plume of blue

smoke. Clarence said, "Now let I and I partake of this Inscience." Meaning, let's have a smoke. Rastafarians are the most voluble stoned rappers in the world. An articulate Rasta will drop a lengthy sermon at the slightest provocation. Heavy religious testimony is routinely carried on at a level of regular conversation that would shame any holy-rolling fundamentalist Christian sect. Clarence tried to explain it:

"First there is the Imperial I, who is called Haile-I Selassie-I. Then there is the I-wah, which represents the unending spiritual time of Jah Rastafari. And there is the I-ree, which is the time which all men pass through. And then there is I, which you will take to mean myself. And there is I and I, which is myself and all the Rasta brethren and even you. As in *Let I and I partake of this Inscience,* which refers specifically to this herb here. Did I tell it too fast for I? It's easy. This Inscience lead to good Iditation, which bring on the Ivinity of a mon . . ." One realizes eventually that Rasta imagery is much like Blakeian imagery; to understand, all you need is the key.

Rasta, Clarence says, is struggling for the soul of the nation. Asked what he and the Rastafarian Idren (brethren) think of the political terror currently being waged in Kings-ton, Clarence dips the bamboo pipe again, lights it, murmurs, "Give thanks," and intones simply, "Kingston is at its *best.*" The bulging, exalted eyes fix the visitor hard for a moment, and you get the drift of what he means.

Marcus Garvey words come to pass/Marcus Garvey words come to pass/Can't get no food to eat/Can't get no money to spend.

In Roots the trio known as Burning Spear is chanting and trance-rocking, backed by a lean, reckless young band whose guitarist is chopping off notes like fish heads, knifing through the grotto-dark smoky club until the swaying customers at the packed tables feel their nervous systems being slightly realigned. *Do you remember the days of slavery?* Burning Spear himself, the lead singer and one of the major reggae seers, is wearing a Rootsman University shirt under crisp army fatigues fitted with Ethiopian patches of red, green, and gold. His eyes are closed and he's stepping off as he chants. He looks deep jet, like a Togolese hardwood fetish come to life. His hair is beginning to turn to locks. Under the chanting and the blitz from Spear's pickup group, the Truth Defender Band, the brains of the audience are beginning to turn into mangoes.

Alaric

Clarence, Alaric, Kiddus-I

Burning Spear is the newest of the major reggae stars, and is perhaps the best loved group in Jamaica. Their recording of a song called "Marcus Garvey" caught Jamaicans in 1974 with its blistering attack, martial horns, and unabashedly ethnic singing. "Marcus Garvey" reminded people of the Jamaican roots of their national hero and prophet and again called attention to the suffering and poverty of the slums. The song was a scream in the night from the ghetto, and Jamaicans understood its power. Another single, "Slavery Days," was as hypnotic as it was poignant. Burning Spear's major influence was African song rather than rhythm and blues. Spear's music seemed to transcend all labels but "primitive"; their antiphonal chanting could have come from Cameroon or antebellum Louisiana were it not for the electric stimuli of the Truth Defenders. Burning Spear sings no songs of love and sex. They are a political, nationalist, Rasta propaganda machine and let all the contradictions evanesce into the night. They take their name from the Burning Spear of Kenya, Jomo Kenyatta, the Mau Mau himself. They've been singing since 1969, when lead singer Winston Rodney and bass singer Rupert Willington began recording as a duo for Sir Coxone. Later they were joined by first tenor Delroy Hines. They left Coxone in 1971 after a dozen of their tribal chants had been released to little acclaim. Spear recorded "Marcus Garvey" for the sound system run by an Ocho Rios entrepreneur named Jack Ruby.

At first Ruby only played the track on his system, but its popularity almost forced him to release it as a single. Soon after, Sir Coxone issued three of his Spear singles ("Ethiopia Live It Out," "Swell Head," and "Foggy Road"), and Jamaica was gripped by Spear-mania.

Since then there's been two albums and more singles, and Winston Rodney is recognized as a shaman in the same class as Bob Marley, a powerful musician who can hypnotize a crowd with his piercing voice and hard-edged, unrepentant music. This night at Roots he cooks for three hours with one fifteen-minute break for a spliff, working through "Marcus Garvey," "Tradition" (based on an old St. Ann obeah song—Spear's from St. Ann and he rarely leaves the parish), "The Invasion," "Slavery Days," "Jordan River," "Give Me (Free Access)," and a dozen or so

more. Every song is arranged to first embrace the listener with tension and apprehension, and then to release him via hypnotic repetition. At the end of a reprise of "Marcus Garvey" the three Spears crouch into a little mojo shakedown, and then Hines and Willington slack-step offstage, leaving Rodney, thirty years old but suddenly looking ninety, arrow-straight in his dripping fatigues under the spotlight. *"JAH,"* he yells, *"RASTAFARI!"* And the lights go out.

A bit later I went up to the musicians' room to see if I could talk with Winston Rodney for a moment. But when I got to the top of the stairs the door to the room flung open and a semicomatose Burning Spear, staggering and barely on his feet, lurched forward supported by a pair of his retainers. After the night's per-

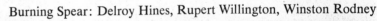

Burning Spear: Delroy Hines, Rupert Willington, Winston Rodney

Burning Spear in the studio

formance there was nothing left of him, and he looked like a gnarled medicine man after some arcane purification rite. Jack Ruby, short, swarthy, and barrel-chested, charged out after them and said he'd be back with some of his people the next day. In the musicians' room Clarence and Alaric were still dipping their pipe. "Ites," they said amiably. "Iree. Give thanks!"

Reggae musicians are organized as traditional musical brotherhoods, each with its own chief, master musician, jester, drummers, a priest. The brotherhood has rules and a language of its own, an informal star system, and a fixed set of opinions, rivalries, jealousies. One or more of the better instrumentalists may also be associated with several other brotherhoods.

Jack Ruby is more or less the typical chief of a typical reggae brotherhood. His real name is Lawrence Lindo; his *nom de musique* comes from his days as a waiter in the Ocho Rios resorts. Lindo used to call his colleagues Jackson, and during the events of the first Kennedy assassination the moniker was turned around and perversely shortened to Jack Ruby. His fortunes as a small-time sound-system man changed when Burning Spear fell into his lap, and now the proud Ruby is producer and godfather to a pride of reggae lions.

Reggae musicians tend to be either singers or players, and within the brotherhoods there are two distinct tribes—the vocal trios, such as Burning Spear and (in Ruby's case) Justin Hines and the Dominoes and Righteous Foundation; and the backing bands. Ruby has one of the best, a crack platoon of studio musicians headed by the prolific guitarist Earl "Chinna" Smith and bassist Robbie Shake-

The Black Disciples at Chela Bay

Top, from left: Herman Marquis, Burning Spear, Bobby Ellis, Philip Fullwood, Jack Ruby
Bottom, from left: Dirty Harry Hall, Vincent "Trommy" Gordon,
Robbie Shakespeare, Noel Skully Sims, Leroy Horsemouth Wallace, Earl "Chinna" Smith, Delroy Hines

speare. In addition, every tribe has its complement of herbsmen and camp followers and hopeful young musicians trying to get a break from the chief in the form of a chance to record a single.

The morning after Burning Spear's night at Chela Bay, Ruby showed up at the hotel, having cannily rounded up the members of his tribe from the Kingston and Ocho Rios areas with promises of press coverage and a cockfight. Since Chela Bay had the only live reggae on the island, it had drawn almost every foreign journalist in Jamaica that weekend, from the rock press to dour straight-men from Time Inc. On these worthies Ruby unchained his crew and soon the verandas chimed with much bawdy yukking and the

clink of Red Stripe bottles. The drummer Leroy Horsemouth Wallace wore a slinky red satin jump suit and a black pimp's hat and pulled off the wig of Skully Sims just as a *Time* photographer was snapping Sims' portrait. Burning Spear, somewhat recovered from the previous night's exertions, permitted his picture to be taken and chatted intently with his lyricist, a Dread named Philip Fullwood. Touter, or Bernard Harvey, a keyboardist who used to play with the Wailers, was rolling spliffs. The great reggae horn men (who are constantly accused of playing out of tune) stood somberly having their pictures taken. Justin Hines, an excellent singer who had started in the ska days, came in with his retinue. As it started to rain lightly, Ruby herded

Jack Ruby

everyone under a porch to hear his new group, Righteous Foundation, who crouched with hand drums and guitars and sang a beautiful tune with perfect ensemble harmonies. When it was through there was a rolling crash of sheet lightning and everyone smiled uneasily and looked at the sky. There was no need for applause.

After a while the photographers ran out of film and the foreign writers lapsed into narcolepsy from the ganja they had ingested. Ruby decided it was time for the cockfight, which the assembled players anticipated with relish. It was late in the afternoon as Ruby sauntered down the wet road; the sky had lifted and the sun was burning gold through the clouds. As he walked Ruby was pestered for some cash to bet with by Rupert Willington, the statue-faced Spear singer. Ruby and Willington got involved in a bantering argument about who

Righteous
Foundation

Robbie Shakespeare and Yubby Youth

Righteous Foundation Jamming at Chela Bay

owed how much to whom, spiced liberally with menstrual curses—*Blood clot! Ras clot, anyway!* Finally the young musician cadged a two-dollar bill and when the razor-sharp spikes were strapped on the fighting cocks in the humid pit, Willington put the deuce on a buff slit-eyed cock who turned out to be a bleeder and was cut to feathers within minutes.

That night a group called Ras Michael and the Sons of Negus were supposed to play at the Roots Club, but they didn't show, and the guests had their choice between the bar at the Playboy Club or smoking and talking gibberish all night with the local Dreads. The next day a couple of jalopies screeched to a breathless halt outside the hotel, and a half-dozen down-in-the-mouth Rastas announced they were the Sons of Negus, that they had a hit single, and they were ready to play that night. Told that the date was the previous night and they had missed it, they appeared crestfallen. Ras Michael, who seemed pretty urgent, gave some of the press a mini-lecture on the Old Testament, while a drummer, who introduced himself as Kiddus-I, launched into a political tirade against the black and white oppressors. No one had ever heard of Ras Michael and the Sons of Negus, and a couple of the Sons were dressed in rags, but the press dutifully recorded the raps and took the photographs.

After the tape recorders were shut off and the cameras put away, Ras Michael started leaning on the press to share the wealth. He explained his band was poor and needed a camera and a cassette recorder. Michael came on pretty strong, and most of the reporters got disgusted and told him to fuck off and hoped his fellow players were as wiped out as they looked and wouldn't pick up a machete. One American photographer finally weakened under the pressure and bestowed upon the ungrateful Ras Michael a broken Polaroid. With that the Sons of Negus roared off back to Kingston in their jalopies, but not before a toothless drummer named Ras Sidney asked me to send him an oboe when I got back to the states. Who *are* the Sons of Negus?

Out west of Ocho Rios, on the road to Runaway Bay, there's a Rasta wicker weaver named Bongo Sylly, who has lived for years between the road and the sea in a house he wove from palm, bamboo, and grasses. Just down the road is famous Dunn's River Falls, scene of cigarette commercials and obese tourists scrambling about the misty rocks all day.

Bongo Sylly's been around for a long time and his locks fall to the middle of his back. He's dressed in his vision of Ethiopian splendor and his eyes sometimes seem focused beyond the asteroid belt. He does not roll a spliff as much as weave it, entwining flowers, leaves, seeds, branches of ganja into a huge paper cone, lighting it with a stick from the fire and intoning, "Give thanks Jah Rastafari give thanks Imperial I." Bongo Sylly chews on the spliff for twenty minutes until it's a distractingly soggy black mess, and then he hands it to you. You don't want any, but Bongo Sylly is extremely Dread and usually doesn't even put up with visitors unless they're bringing him presents or money. You can't refuse the spliff, so you just sort of kiss it gingerly. If Bongo Sylly, it is told, walked through Trench Town in his robes, the people would worship him as a saint.

Later Sylly (short for Sylvester) stands on the dark roadside as you say farewell. He is very grave tonight. "Don't write no joke," he says, "or nothing about Jamaica for the sportin' page. You should not say that Jamaica is full of happy folks or fookery like that. Write it out that we are in *pain* here. Ras clot! Write it out that we are in prison and we want to go home."

Bongo Sylly

5

The Brotherhood of Rastafari

It's doubtful that even the most inspired, brain-fevered ethnofantasist could have imagined a construct of beliefs as strange and powerful as those of the Rastafarians. In Jamaica today the Brotherhood of Rastafari is not just a millenarian sect waiting to go back to Africa but an alternative spiritual nationality that supplies a mass cultural identity for thousands of young Jamaicans stranded between their school years and an endless cycle of demeaning labor and unemployment. For the estimated 75,000 Rastas in Jamaica the beliefs and rituals of Rastafari resolve all the killing ironies of a white man's god in a brutalized colonial society. Rasta asceticism allows poor people to make their way through the mechanical detritus of the twentieth century with dignity instead of shame and envy. And, most important, although they are widely thought of as pariah outcasts who reject the material world, the Rastas have been the prevailing cultural force in Jamaica for twenty years, and are the major influence over young Jamaicans

these days. Most of the reggae musicians are Rastas, though not all wear the Gorgonian Dreadlocks that usually identify a Rasta brother. Many of the island's best actors and painters are committed Rastas as well.

If it weren't for reggae, few people would have heard of Rasta. Visitors to Jamaica have long been warned that the menacing devils with snake nests for hair would disembowel them and eat their livers at the slightest provocation. But reggae, especially the music of the Wailers, has thrust the Rasta cosmology into the middle of the planet's cultural arenas, and suddenly people want to know what all the chanting and praying and obsessive smoking of herb are all about.

Everyone in Jamaica has an opinion of Rastafari. The middle and upper classes think of Rastas as violent hippies who should be wiped out. The government tolerates and tries to use them to its political advantage. The police wage limited war on it. But every year Rasta accumulates more prestige in Jamaican life.

Greg Russell

Skilly Cole

One night a young engineer put it to me this way: "For years Jamaicans feared the Rasta as a voluntary ascetic who didn't vote and just smoked herb all day long. Then, after many years, people realized that the Rastas have contributed *more* to Jamaican culture than any other group. In time, they've become the conscience of the country. We feel we need them more than they need us."

Rasta starts with Marcus Garvey.

He was born in 1887 in St. Ann's Bay. His father was a stonemason descended from the Maroon tribes, the independent nation of runaway slaves deep in the island's interior. When Garvey was fifteen he left for Kingston, where a few years later he became involved with radical journalism espousing the Back-to-Africa movement. At the age of twenty he led a bitter printers' strike although he was the shop foreman and technically on management's side. In Kingston he gained some small fame as a preacher and amateur entrepreneur. He ar-

Marcus Garvey, Harlem, 1924

rived in the United States in 1916 and the following year founded the Universal Negro Improvement Association, originally as a fraternal organization, later remolding it to become the organized vehicle for the redemption of blacks through repatriation to Africa. In New York he started a newspaper, *The Negro World,* which took as its motto Garvey's black nationalist rallying cry—One Aim, One God, One Destiny. Through most of 1919–20, Garvey, a compact, fiery man with penetrating eyes and a booming preacher's voice, traveled over America, spreading UNIA doctrine and being hailed as a savior by every black community he visited.

Some say that Marcus Garvey was a prophet. Others say he was a hustler. Marcus Moziah Garvey was possessed by an amazing entrepreneurial drive. In 1919 he founded a steamship company, the Black Star Line, which would "link the colored peoples of the world in commercial and industrial discourse." Purchase of stock was limited to blacks, and Garvey raised millions of dollars selling single shares at five dollars apiece to believers in his ideas of black pride and redemption. It is said that Garvey didn't intend, as his critics claimed, that the Black Star Line would eventually provide transportation back to Africa for those who wanted to go. But the publicity angle of that belief was put to profitable use by the company's fundraisers. Despite constant harassment by federal and New York authorities, the line purchased an old cotton freighter, renamed it the S.S. *Frederick Douglass,* and began trading between New York and Jamaica in 1920.

The same year Garvey convened a worldwide convention of the UNIA which dazzled the City of New York. Thousands of Garveyites paraded through Harlem in colorful uniforms. The main sessions in Madison Square Garden were attended by African chieftains in full regalia. Issuing an international proclamation of anticolonialism and African nationalism, Garvey thundered from the rostrum, "We are the descendants of a suffering people. We are the descendants of a people determined to suffer no longer." Harlem tobacco shops sold Marcus Garvey cigars with the prophet's picture on the band. There was a popular race recording of a song called "Black Star Line." The streets of black communities

in New York, Chicago, and St. Louis rang to the UNIA anthem, "Ethiopia Thou Land of Our Fathers."

Garvey had become in his mid-thirties the strongest and most feared black in America. In 1922 he was so confident of his position that he met with the hierarchy of the Ku Klux Klan in Louisiana to discuss KKK support for African repatriation. But the following year his troubles began. Poor management forced the Black Star Line into bankruptcy. Garvey was tried for mail fraud and tax evasion, was convicted, and sent to federal prison in 1925. His sentence was commuted by Calvin Coolidge in 1927, and Garvey was deported to Panama.

Marcus made his way back to Jamaica,

Haile Selassie at coronation, 1930

ONE GOD ONE AIM, ONE DESTINY

where he revived the UNIA and held several spectacular theatrical UNIA conventions that older Jamaicans remember as the most glorious sights they ever witnessed. Garvey stepped up his pulpit prophecies, predicting full repatriation for New World blacks by 1960. Garvey's nationalism wasn't well received by colonial authorities, and he lived the rest of his life in England, where he died of pneumonia in 1940.

Back in 1924, the UNIA attempted to establish a repatriated black colony in Liberia but was rebuffed by the Liberian Government. Marcus Garvey died without ever setting foot in Africa. But in the Kenya of the 1920s Garvey's message was getting through, and young men like Jomo Kenyatta were listening very carefully. From the lessons of Marcus Garvey came the nationalist movements that would one day force Africa back into the hands of Africans. In 1952, Garvey was proclaimed a national hero by Jamaica.

In a Kingston church one Sunday in 1927, Marcus Garvey prophesied, "Look to Africa, where a black king shall be crowned, for the day of deliverance is here."

In 1930 a tribal warlord from a remote corner of Ethiopia named Ras Tafari Makonnen had himself crowned the 111th Emperor of Ethiopia in a line traced to the union of King Solomon and Queen Makeda of Sheba. His new title was King of Kings, Lord of Lords, His Imperial Majesty the Conquering Lion of the Tribe of Judah, Elect of God. Tafari took a new name: Haile Selassie— "Power of the Holy Trinity."

Jamaican Garveyites saw the picture of the new African emperor on the front page of the *Daily Gleaner* and consulted their Bibles for a sign. Could this be the black king of whom Garvey preached? The textual evidence was strong. Revelation 5:2,5: "And I saw a strong angel proclaiming with a loud voice, 'Who is worthy to open the Book, and to loose the seals thereof?' . . . And one of the elders saith unto me, 'Weep not: behold, the Lion of

SELASSIE: WHAT LIFE HAS TAUGHT ME

Tuesday, April 28, 1964 CALIFORNIA:

What life has taught me on the question of racial discrimination I like to share with those who want to learn:

That until the philosophy which holds one race superior and another inferior is finally and permanently discredited and abandoned;

That until there are no longer first-class and second class citizens of any nation;

That until the colour of a man's skin is of no more significance than the colour of his eyes;

That until the basic human rights are equally guaranteed to all, without regard to race;

That until that day, the dream of lasting peace and world citizenship and the rule of international morality will remain in but a fleeting illusion to be pursued but never attained;

And until the ignoble and unhappy regimes that hold our brothers in Angola, in Mozambique and in South Africa in sub-human bondage have been toppled and destroyed;

Until bigotry and prejudice and malicious and inhuman self-interest have been replaced by understanding and tolerance and goodwill;

Until all Africans stand and speak as free beings, equal in the eyes of the Almighty;

Until that day, the African continent will not know peace. We Africans will fight, if necessary and we know that we shall win, as we are confident in the victory of good over evil.

Judah, the Root of David, hath prevailed to open the Book, and to loose the seven spirits of God sent forth into all the earth."

Several preachers in Kingston began to pray to Haile Selassie as the living God and the central figure of African redemption. Worshipers of Selassie became known as Ras Tafaris, or Rastamen. After an account was published in the Kingston press describing the Niyabinghi Order (which was formed in the Congo and Ethiopia in the mid-1930s to overthrow colonialism through racial war), some of the Rastas took to calling themselves Niyamen. The most successful of the Rasta preachers was L. P. Howell, who sold thousands of small portraits of Selassie for a shilling each, telling his customers that it was their passport to Ethiopia. The police reacted by committing Howell and every Rasta they could arrest to terms in mental asylums on charges of lunacy.

When Howell got out of the asylum in 1940, he acquired an old estate deep in the mountains, called Pinnacle, and moved there with 1500 Rasta followers from Kingston and Morant Bay. There Howell established himself

as Selassie's regent in Jamaica, living with his wives and a praetorian guard of "Ethiopian Warriors." Ganja was the main cash crop. From the earliest days Rastas had worn long hair and beards because of the Old Testament admonitions that no razor shall touch the head of the faithful. At Howell's Rasta camp at Pinnacle the long hair was plaited into dangling locks after the Rastas saw pictures of the hairdos of Masai and Somali soldiers from East Africa. They became known as Locksmen, or Dreadlocks. (Dread is a term that denotes the irreconcilable point between the Rasta and authority, used as a noun, adjective, or expletive.) It is said the first Dreadlocks began to appear in 1947.

In 1954 the police finally raided Pinnacle and closed it down. Howell's Rastas had become violent in response to their leader's demands, raiding their neighbors and looting other farmers' ganja crops. There were thousands of Rastas occupying the land, which Howell had been running like a Maroon nation, an autonomous state within a state. With Pinnacle no longer a haven, many Rastas moved to Kingston, and the spread of the movement dates from then.

Rastafari brethren profess no monolithic creed. Some Rastas wear their hair in locks, while others wear it short. Some smoke copious amounts of ganja, while others shun it.

Laws Street, Kingston

Some Rastas avoid all work, while others are Jamaica's finest woodcarvers, artists, and craftsmen. Only two beliefs hold the brethren in common: that Ras Tafari is the living God, and that redemption for the black man can come only through repatriation to Africa. The great majority of Rastas are vegetarians, avoiding meat and shellfish. Pork eaters are especially despised by Dreads. Processed food is suspect by most Rastas, who prefer "I-tal" (real or natural) food—grains, fruit, roots, and vegetables.

Rastas think of themselves as the lost tribes of Israel sold into the slavery of a Caribbean Babylon, and when the children of Israel fly away home to Zion at last, the throne of Babylon—colonial Jamaica and the whole of white civilization—will tumble down in a hail

of blood and brimstone. Careful attention is paid to esoteric biblical texts to justify the Rasta cosmology, and arcane Rasta oral history explains what the Bible neglects. So a Dread after a couple of spliffs will tell you that the black race sinned in primeval days and was punished by Jah in the form of the conquest and enslavement of Africa by white men. The four great pirates (John Hawkins, Cecil Rhodes, Stanley Livingstone, and U. S. Grant) brought the slaves to the New World to enrich the Babylonian Queen Elizabeth I, currently reincarnate as Elizabeth II. The golden Scepter of the House of Judah in Ethiopia, magically empowered with the dominion of the world, was stolen from Ethiopia by Marc An-

tony and Julius Caesar, who used it to build the Roman Empire. From Rome the Scepter was stolen by Britain, which inherited the Roman world. When Haile Selassie was crowned in 1930, King George V of England sent his son, the Duke of Gloucester, to Ethiopia with the Scepter as a gift to the Emperor. While he was in Ethiopia the Duke became drunk and wandered off in the wilderness and ate tall grass, revealing himself to be the reincarnate King of Babylon, Nebuchadnezzar. When the Duke gave Selassie the Scepter, the Emperor regained his powers. Selassie sent a mysterious emblem back to England with the Duke to give to his father, but when King George saw the emblem he was paralyzed and died shortly

after. Gloucester became king and, to fulfill the prophecies, abdicated in the knowledge that he would resume the throne after the reincarnate Elizabeth I to rule as the final king of Babylon and preside over its utter destruction.

Rastas say that in its local Jamaican form Babylon is represented by the government, the police, and the church. Most Rastas refuse to vote or pay taxes or send their children to school. (Ironically there is a Haile Selassie grade school—donated by the Emperor—in Kingston that refuses to accept children wearing dreadlocks.) They say it is sinful for women to wear cosmetics, and a Rasta will not lie with a woman who is menstruating. In fact the entire Rasta system of curses is based on a traditional fear of the menstrual cycle. *Blood clot* is bad. *Ras clot* is worse. *Bumba clot* is terrible. Calling someone a *pussy clot* is fair grounds for having your neck opened with a machete. Alcohol, especially rum, is forbidden as an insidious Babylonian technique of mass murder and insanity. The Bible urges the children of Rastafari to smoke cannabis in Genesis 8, Psalm 18 and Revelation 22. All forms of Jamaican witchcraft and Christian revivalism are viewed with contempt as unforgivable superstition that detracts from the mystic revelation of Rastafari.

Rastafarians became known as a violent cult shortly after Pinnacle was closed down in 1954. Locksmen moved their camps into Trench Town and the Dungle and a crime wave began. With an estimated twenty thousand country people migrating to Kingston every year, the lure of Rasta at first provided an alternative to limbo and protest in the slums. After the Rude Boy phenomenon faded out, many former Rudies became Rastas, or at least they grew their locks. (It is often said of a phony Rasta that "Him have locks on head but not in heart.") In 1959 Rasta street riots provoked a formal study on the cult by Kingston's University of the West Indies, which

made several recommendations to the government on behalf of the Rastas. But police equated the Rastafarians with the ganja trade, and where once Rastas had been committed to mental hospitals without clinical diagnostic evidence, in the early '60s brethren who dared to flash their locks on the street disappeared into jail. In 1963 a group of Rastas let the pressure get to them and hacked up a gas station attendant in Coral Gardens, near Montego Bay. Then they burned the gas station, sacked a motel, killed a Jamaican guest, and generally went berserk until subdued by the army. Hundreds of Dreadlocks were rounded up and jailed, and to the mass of Jamaicans Rastafari became synonymous with terror and Rude Boyism. Three Coral Gardens Rastas were hanged.

Now that many of the Rastafarian ideas have passed on to the younger generation of Jamaicans at large, Rastas take pains to prove they are nonviolent and say they want only to go home to Africa. Rasta groups like the Ethiopians croon "Carry me back to Ethiopia" and espouse quiescence and harmony. Prince Talice had a hit with "Decent Citizen," while Levi Williams soothes the airwaves with "Peaceful Rasta."

In the late '50s, several Jamaican families actually moved to Ethiopia, occupying farmland donated by Haile Selassie. But after several years the group deteriorated in doctrinal disputes and several Rastas were actually deported back to Jamaica by Ethiopian authorities. Selassie dissolved the commission he had created to study resettlement in Ethiopia of Caribbean blacks. The Emperor is reported to have stated the last thing his country needed was thousands of lazy drug addicts who didn't pay their taxes.

As a godhead, Haile Selassie didn't cut such a bad figure. On his way to the throne he had found it expedient to execute many of his rivals, and the Empress of Ethiopia died mysteriously just before Selassie's succession to the throne. But Selassie was determined to

Haile Selassie, 1970

push his Stone Age kingdom into the nineteenth century, at least, and in 1923, Ethiopia was admitted to the League of Nations at Geneva. After his coronation the Lion of Judah embarked on a royal progress of the European capitals, accompanied by a half-dozen of the royal lions and several pet cheetahs. When the Jamaican Rastafarians heard about the lions, they went into paroxysms of awe and worship.

In 1935, Mussolini's Italian Army invaded Ethiopia, and Haile Selassie made his legendary plea for help from the League of Nations. Soon after, a picture appeared in the *Daily Gleaner* of Selassie standing on a huge unexploded Italian bomb, which was taken for a great miracle by the Rastas. The Italian invasion of Ethiopia seemed to confirm the prophecy of Revelation 19:19: "And I saw the Beast, and the kings of the earth gathered together to make war on him that sat on the throne." With Selassie's triumphant return to Ethiopia (engineered by Winston Churchill in 1941), the succeeding verse was fulfilled: "And the Beast was taken, and with him the false prophet that wrought miracles before him, with which he deceived them that had the mark of the Beast, and them that worshipped his image."

Selassie was mercurial, alternately playful and somber. Visiting European diplomats would find him toying with his house lions, thrusting his head between their open jaws in demonstration of their love and docility. In 1963 he sponsored the establishment of the nationalist Organization of African Unity and built its headquarters in Addis Ababa. He rode through the desiccated streets of his capital in a maroon Rolls-Royce, tossing bundles of paper money to his prostrate subjects. He was capable of letting thousands of Ethiopians starve in times of famine, too proud to let international relief agencies report on Ethiopian crop devastation for fear he would lose respect in Europe. He surrounded himself with the most corrupt officialdom in recent African history.

In 1966, Haile Selassie was invited to make a state visit to Jamaica by Michael Manley, the son of Jamaica's leading politician and the current Prime Minister of Jamaica. Although Manley's party was not then in power in Jamaica, the ruling party, the Jamaica Labourites, thought that if Selassie would come to the island and deny his divinity, the burgeoning Rasta movement would be defused and all the foolish talk about going back to Africa would stop.

On April 21, 1966, thousands of Rastas and Dreadlocks were waiting at Kingston's Palisadoes Airport. Many had come from all over the island and had literally been waiting for weeks. According to Rasta legend, that morning a solitary white dove flew over the massed Rastas, followed by a short, gentle rain shower of benediction. Selassie's jet flew in from the east, out of the dawn, and when the Imperial Lion was seen on the fuselage a great cheer went up from the crowd. The plane came to a halt and thousands of Dreads broke through police lines and ran to the plane. Hundreds crouched in the shade cast by the imperial wings and lighted their chalices—huge flamboyant goat's-horn waterpipes filled with ganja. Selassie walked through the door, stood on the top of the ramp, and beheld ten thousand Dreads crushed around his plane, smoking, chanting, praising his name, and falling on their foreheads. He took one long look, turned around, walked back into his plane, and had the door shut. For another hour the Emperor refused to come out.

The Dreads had pushed the official welcoming delegation out of reach of Selassie, effecting what has come to be called "the capture of ceremonies." The ceremonial red carpet that the Emperor was to have trod was destroyed by Rastas who claimed it was a "rug of colonialism," since Queen Elizabeth had used it during an earlier state visit. The Dread master Mortimer Planner finally knocked on the door of the jet and prevailed upon the Emperor to show himself. When the Dreads saw Selassie, they again went wild at the visage of the Imperial I, and commenced a chanting that went on for days. Says one Rasta elder, "Everything that day was totally free. The expression of the people was love in its totality. Right under the wing of that plane the brethren sat and strike matches and lit the chalice. You see, the reality of that free Ireets was within that Iwa. There was no fear that day. There was nothing to fear. With the love of Jah there is no need to fear his power. It was a total blessing for us all." Other Dread elders back in Trench Town, too advanced in ganja use to attend the airport reception, grumbled that if Selassie were really God he wouldn't have needed a plane to fly to Jamaica.

Everywhere Selassie went in Jamaica he was received with crazed displays of affection and loyalty. A motion was offered in Parliament to make him King of Jamaica. The headlines of the day read "SAVAGE JOY SWAMPS SELASSIE," and "A WILD WELCOME FOR NEGUS." Most importantly, prominent Rasta elders were henceforth included in official ceremonies for the Emperor, the first time that temporal authority ever conceded anything to the Brotherhood of Rastafari. In a speech Selassie denied his divinity but the Dreads didn't care; the prophecy could not be gainsaid.

Rastafarians and the police are still carrying on an undeclared state of war, as we discovered one afternoon when we were giving a ride to several Dreads from Bob Marley's tribe, including Seeco Patterson, the Wailers' hand drummer. We came to a traffic jam on Slipe Road, the central avenue in downtown Kingston. A half-dozen police were checking cars for ganja and illegal weapons. As we moved slowly by several police sharks gingerly cradling machine guns in their arms, Peter Simon raised his camera to squeeze off a quick photo and the shutter of his Nikon cracked like an M-16 misfiring and startled the sharks, who seemed to go into a feeding frenzy. Six gun barrels came up in unison and pointed at us. The squad leader leaned over and stuck his head in the car. When he saw the three Dreads in the back seat he wrinkled his nose in disgust. "Dis car smell *wicked!* Get out with hands behind head! Leave everything in cyaar!" There was no one over the rank of private. The squad leader wore a pullover so you couldn't see his badge, and the numbers had been ripped off their caps. The squad leader was popeyed and illiterate; he tried to read the driver's license upside down. It was a classic, typical Jamaican roadblock, the kind of police terror you might've heard about in the Wailers' "Three O'Clock Road Block" but perhaps didn't really think conceivable.

A few minutes later the Kingston police arrived and dismissed the sharks, who turned out to be paramilitary vigilante troops. After the police and the squad leader argued and swore at each other in dialect over jurisdiction at this particular roadblock, the police frisked everybody and started to search the car. Officers poked and humiliated the Rastas. One Dread was told to remove his fatigue jacket because a Rasta wearing fatigues was an insult to the army. It was something like a posse of

Three O'clock Roadblock

drunk Wyoming state troopers ragging a car-load of hippies in 1966. The police ridiculed the Dreadlocks and their religion and spit on them. Finally the sergeant finished his exasperated futile search of our car. "Dis a *bumba clot!* I can even *smell* the herb you been smokin'." One of the Dreads was bold enough to argue with the sergeant, saying that soon herb would be legal and the police would be poor again. The furious sergeant looked at me and said, "Ganja dirty, dirty like these Rasta clots. Ya don't have no business with this kind, mon."

I assumed there was going to be a plant.

Dread with chalice at Cascade

The police had searched the car and all three Rastas with great caution but found nothing, and they let us go. On the way back to Marley's house one of the Dreads seemed to pull out his herb from thin air and roll a spliff.

"Now," said Niya, "now white man knows what it's like. Can see how police violence is the cause of so much hate. Can see why Rasta must go home soon."

The I-vine Theocratic Majesty Haile Selassie died in a small apartment in his former palace in Addis Ababa on August 27, 1975. A few months earlier the impatient young colonels of his army overthrew the Selassie regime in a coup, humiliated the Emperor, and accused him of treason for letting a hundred thousand peasants die of neglect during the worst drought in Ethiopia's recorded history.

The colonels held Selassie in his former palace, hoping to trade his life for the billions they claimed he had stashed away in Swiss banks. He was reviled as a thief and a tyrant who had become fabulously wealthy on the backs of the poorest people in the world. The colonels would have liked to execute him, but they were superstitious and fearful of his power, even as a frail, broken prisoner. Selassie's supporters in exile whispered that the Emperor's nurse had been slowly poisoning his soup.

In Jamaica, they laughed at the Rastas and taunted that their God had died. But Rastas give no credence to death and went on as usual. Bob Marley wrote a song and the Wailers recorded it. "Jah Live" was released as a single and became overnight the biggest-selling record in reggae's history. The beat was slow and the I-Threes melted down into a disconsolate moan, but the words were full of affirmation and life:

> Jah Live!
> Children, yeah
> Jah Jah live
> Children, yeah
> Its a foolish dog
> Barks at a flying bird
> What sheep must learn, children
> To respect the Shepherd
> Fools saying in their heart
> Rasta, your God is dead
> But I and I know
> Dread shall be dread and dread
> Jah Live!

Laws Street, Kingston

MAN JUMPS IN LIONS' CAGE, KILLED

A man was bitten to death yesterday evening when he jumped into the lions' cage at Hope Botanical Gardens, Kingston 6, for the second time for the day.

Up to last night the body of the man was still in the cage but locked off from the lions as it waited to be transported to the morgue.

The deceased who, as a zoo spokesman said, appeared to be mentally ill, had not been identified.

According to reports he first jumped into the lions' cage in the morning but was quickly rescued from Leo and Liz and their three cubs by attendants. Zoo officials treated him for a cut to the hand.

To a zoo employee who sought a reason for his invasion of the cage, he replied: "I dead already."

Shortly after he was released, a worker, attracted by sounds of "Lord have mercy" rushed to the lions' cage to find the man being devoured by Leo and Liz. . . .

Daily Gleaner
January 3, 1976

6

Three Reggae Masters

Jimmy Cliff lives in a suburban house on Lady Musgrave Road, not unlike the ritzy place a struggling and desperate Ivan O. Martin was chased away from in *The Harder They Come* when he went seeking odd jobs in the lush gardens. The house is London resident Cliff's Jamaican headquarters, but its rooms are completely bare but for carpeting, a bed, a chair or two. It's still the home of someone who's done well, but its owner doesn't seem to feel completely at ease, as if he maintained the house as his link to his roots but preferred his flat in Earl's Court. Since 1965, Jimmy Cliff —reggae master, soul singer, movie star, devout Muslim—has lived in England, still reaching for the acclaim that would have been denied him had he stayed home. All the signs read that Cliff is about to break the cycle of success and disappointment that has ruled his life thus far. Four years after his portrayal of the archetypal Ivan pushed Jimmy into the ground zero of reggae enthusiasm, he is an established star in England and Europe, has a solid American recording contract, and has es-

tablished a toehold in Mother Africa, where he is the biggest selling singer in Ghana and Nigeria.

Jimmy Cliff was born James Chambers in St. James Parish in 1948. At thirteen he moved to Kingston by himself and survived in the streets hanging around the sound systems, pestering the proprietors to give him a chance. After cutting a bunch of sound-system acetates that were used for dances and never released (only the most wildly popular were ever issued), Cliff finally recorded a single, "Daisy Got Me Crazy," in 1962 at the age of fourteen. This was in pre-ska days, when most Jamaican records were happy rip-offs of American R&B phrases. The big Jamaican stars of the day were Owen Gray (still around and a popular reggae artist), Jackie Morgan, Laural Aitken, Derrick Morgan, and the vocal duo of Joe Higgs and Delroy Wilson. Jimmy Cliff recalls getting no money for his first record and very little for any of the dozens he wrote and recorded before he was twenty-one.

Cliff's first hit, also in 1962, was called

"Dearest Beverley." One day that year Leslie Kong, who with his brothers owned a combination restaurant, ice cream stand, and record shop called Beverley's, was approached by a skinny ambitious kid who claimed to have written a song called "Dearest Beverley." The kid suggested that it would be a good promotion for the Kong enterprise if Leslie went into the recording business. Kong rented a studio, the single was cut, money changed hands, and it went on the radio. Leslie Kong produced Cliff on several other local hits ("My Lucky Day," "Miss Jamaica") until 1965. Kong went on to be a major reggae producer who worked with almost every Jamaican artist until his death in 1971.

In 1965, Cliff became convinced his future lay away from Jamaican music. He moved to London and after a long and difficult period put together a band (mostly young British musicians) and became a popular club act in France and Scandinavia, doing soul routines and a few of his Jamaican sounds in a ska format. He recorded several singles for Island Records, trying to shake off his musical patois and assume a more cosmopolitan soul style. Confused, displaced, and pitifully poor, during this period he wrote his masterpiece, "Many Rivers to Cross," a profoundly emotional epic ballad about depression and getting started again after a bad time. The song was typical Cliff; wretchedness and desolation putting on a good face and trying to look to the future.

Cliff went to Brazil in 1968 as the Jamaican representative at a song festival and ended up working and staying six months. Mingling with the astounding Brazilian cacophony of every conceivable race and color, Cliff produced the tune that became his first international success, "Wonderful World Beautiful People." The next year his low-key but very forceful protest, "Vietnam," was released, much more rock and roll than reggae. A devastating antiwar polemic in the form of a letter to a mother telling of her son's death in Vietnam, the song was too honest and tough to be popular beyond the tiny Cliff cult.

In 1970 Perry Henzell was looking for a singer to play the lead in his untitled film. At first he wanted Johnny Nash, but Nash was unavailable. Henzell then saw a photograph of Cliff on one of his British albums and knew Cliff was what he was looking for, a naïve and sensitive face that could go either way between artist and gangster. Cliff got the part. The movie eventually took its title from the one song Cliff wrote for the film, eager and incurably optimistic, similar to the spirit of "You Can Get It if You Really Want." Characteristically, these two were balanced by "Many Rivers" and the despondent "Sitting in Limbo." The film not only paralleled Cliff's

Jimmy Cliff

life but accurately summed up his personality as well.

Jimmy Cliff is the most misunderstood of the reggae masters. He has been vilified for abandoning his roots and the Jamaican styles that nourished him. His songs continually have described the hunger of a young man trying to assert himself in the face of prejudice and villainy. His stance is self-reliance and independence, and for those qualities he occasionally incurs the wrath of the crowd. In Jamaica, Cliff is respected as an artist who opened doors for reggae that might otherwise have remained shut. Others contend that Cliff moved to England so long ago he's lost contact. Critics point to the smoothness of some

of his recent records, anathema to the fundamentally raw reggae sensibility. His religion gets him into trouble with the Rastafarians. In a weird incident late in 1975 Cliff was spit upon during a Wailers concert in Kingston by Rastas indignant at Cliff's ardent embrace of Islam.

Jimmy Cliff in one sense seems to be listening to his critics. His latest records have been partly recorded in Jamaica with local musicians, and several cuts aim at a chopping, bluesy reggae feel. And when Cliff tours the States and Europe he is propelled by a hand-picked band of Jamaicans that crackle electrically, something like sheet lightning over a St. Ann rain forest on a good night. Reggae master Joe Higgs supports Cliff on timbales

and vocals, and the band is often directed by Augustus Pablo, the top session leader of the Kingston studios these days. Cliff's performances are honed and invariably precise, devoid of any slickness or posturing. The songs in concert tend to be note-for-note as the recorded originals, and I've never witnessed Jimmy Cliff's audience not on its feet and chukking by the end of every show.

We drove up to Jimmy Cliff's house in the middle of a hot afternoon. The tropic fevers had gotten to our driver: as we drew up to the closed iron gate the wrong pedal got pushed and we accelerated and slammed into the iron grillwork. *KRAAAAAAANG.* We drove through, up the long circular driveway, and pulled under an awning. Startled by the crash, Cliff came out to investigate. Embarrassment.

"Yes, mon." Cliff smiled, showing teeth. "We heard your ring."

After posing for a while under a tree playing his guitar, Cliff said he'd rather be portrayed in the ghetto since that was where he was from. He went inside, said goodbye to his shy girlfriend in the kitchen, and we set off taping this interview along Spanish Town Road, where Cliff grew up. On the way we drove around Trench Town trying to find an old barber that Jimmy wanted to see because it was where he learned to play guitar. He was obsessed with the barber, and we crisscrossed the same neighborhood for an hour, Cliff muttering that he knew it was around here somewhere, or at least it *used* to be. . . . When we got to Cliff's old house the sign said *Beware of Tigers and Bad Dogs.* In the courtyard a hen clucked and dropped a blob on Jimmy's foot. Everyone knew him there, and for the first time he seemed at ease.

"I'm from Somerton, which is a little village in St. James, twelve miles from Montego Bay.

Beware of Tigers and Bad Dogs; Jimmy Cliff visiting his old home on Spanish Town Road

I went to school there until I was thirteen and a half, and then I come to Kingston where I live alone, no relatives at all in Kingston. I came because, um, y'know you're supposed to quit school in Jamaica at fourteen years old. I didn't know what I was supposed to do and I had no future at all. What was I supposed to do with my life? Work in a banana field? Cut cane? I came to Kingston to go to night school and learn a trade, but my intention was to sing because I was always singing good in school. My first step in Kingston was to start inquiring about singing.

"First I had an audition, an opportunity at Virgin, it was called, and I won and that was the beginning. I lived in East Kingston for a few months and then went to West Kingston, to Spanish Town Road, where we goin' on. It was violent there, but I wasn't afraid because the environment of Somerton was also tough and I was used to it. You had to know how to defend yourself and fear is a thing you couldn't live with. In West Kingston we had political violence and they tear-gas my house all the time and tear-gas Back O' Wall too. Dem raid and dem tear-gas the whole place. Soon I got to know about ganja and other things that pass through the area. I never needed a gun because I was penetrating the music, y'know. I grew up in an environment that I coulda gone either way, but I chose to do music.

"My first number-one hit was 'Hurricane Hattie.' But before that I had hits on the sound system that never went anywhere. 'Hattie' was about the terrible hurricane we had here in '62. That was with Beverley's, the biggest producer we had before he died—Leslie Kong. I was alone and walking one night, and it was a night of frustrations. So I passed his record shop several times that night and I say, 'Beverly!' Right away I think of a song called

'Beverley' and I walk in there to seduce him with my song that had the same name as his shop. Subliminal seduction, right? I had never been in the business, right? So he liked the song and his brothers were there and they laughed. But Kong didn't laugh, just said it was the best voice he ever heard. In my mind I was saying, *'He's right.'* I was fourteen years old then. He didn't know anything about the business and so I gathered the musicians and two more singers, Monte Morris and Derrick Morgan, got them and bring them in and introduce them. We got a little hit out of 'Hurricane Hattie' and that was the beginning of Leslie Kong, too. But I really did the whole thing. Derrick Morgan I like a lot. 'Fat Man.' 'Rudie in Court.' Dem was big hits. . . .

"*Look,* turn here! This is Trench Town. *Look at that!* When they bulldoze Back O' Wall people were forced to move right in the cemetery. . . .

"So I was recording with Leslie Kong and the hits came up. I stayed with him until I left Jamaica on a trip that was promoting reggae, although it was ska at the time. After many hit records I went to England in '65. I was over there and Perry Henzell sent the script for the movie toward me. I read the script and I liked it because I had known about Rhygin, who was originally a gunman in the '40s. I could identify with him in certain ways. I read the script and said, yeah, I'd like to do it. I went into the movie with big plans. I cannot think small. For the first time I found that I could look at the film objectively in a way I have *never* been able to identify with my music objectively. As an artist, that film was almost my biggest lesson in life.

"The other is my faith. First of all, I'm a Muslim, not a *Black* Muslim. That was just a press word. I consider myself a Muslim like the eight hundred million Muslims all over the world. As I was growing up I was a seeker of the truth. I was first attracted to the Rastafarians because there was a great element of truth in it when I was living in the country. My parents were Christians and that had certain elements of humanity in it, but it wasn't satisfying to me. And so I was always reading and listening carefully. When I went to England I was reading Marx and Engels and politics. But it still wasn't satisfying because I was looking for a root, an identity, a *cause*. I was looking for the cause of the inferiority planted in the so-called black people. But I couldn't find it until I came upon Islam. And then I found out. I came upon Islam about three years ago [1973]. I was into Rasta then deeply, but without locks. My Rasta teacher told me that in the '60s we were supposed to repatriate back to Africa, and the '60s came and the repatriation never came and I became disillusioned. I said I want complete truth, and came to Islam. Now I'm at peace, living and working, and hoping for the best."

Frederick "Toots" Hibbert was born in May Pen, west of Kingston, in the late '40s. In 1961 he moved to Kingston like so many others and hooked up with two other singers —Jerry Mathias and Raleigh Gordon—to form a vocal trio called the Vikings. Toots was the lead singer, Jerry sang low harmony, Raleigh sang high. All three had been raised in church and their first single, "Halleluyah" (released in 1961), was little more than a week-night prayer meeting cut to two and a half minutes and pressed on a record. Soon after, the group changed its name to the Maytals. "Maytals don't mean nothing," Toots admits when pressed. "Jus' sounded good as a name at the time." The word is also supposed to be a combination of May Pen and I-tal.

For more than fifteen years the Maytals have been the prime example of the Jamaican vocal trio. Early on they sang gospel and R&B imitations. When ska was big the Maytals

The Maytals, circa 1967

were a big ska group. When rock-steady took over the Maytals took over rock-steady better than anybody but the Heptones. When reggae evolved Toots took over reggae too, in terms of international exposure and promotion. Except for the Wailers, Toots and the Maytals have been the most prolific exporters of Jamaican music and are perhaps the most widely recognized. They have recorded literally dozens of albums and hundreds of singles, most of them lost and forgotten. Many were made for Coxone Dodd, including the epochal "Six and Seven Books" and "Never Grow Old." Then they went with Prince Buster and had several hits—"Pain in My Belly" was one. Then to Byron Lee, the Jamaican pop bandleader and the owner of Kingston's biggest studio, Dynamic Sound. They stayed in Lee's organization until Toots went to prison in 1966 on a ganja-dealing charge. Out of jail came Toots's most intense song, "5446 Was My Number," a gripping, dangerous litany that graphically describes an armed stickup from the perspective of the prisoner doing time for it. When Toots was freed the group went with Leslie Kong, who produced "Monkey Man" and one of the all-time reggae brain-beaters, "Pressure Drop," a consummate Rudie anthem. Eventually they were signed by Island Records, which cleaned up their unpolished sound to a degree and put them on the road to promote their two albums.

Toots is an eclectic singer and a composer of simple, straight-ahead reggae delivered with an enthused, warbling glee. Of all the Jamaican singers he owes the greatest debt to the American R&B stars from whom he took his main lessons—Otis Redding and especially Sam Cooke. A Maytals show (and there are many of them, since the band has been spending most of its time touring) is part revivalism, part reggae funk, part 1967 Memphis soul review. Toots always starts out with a bored rendition of "Pressure Drop" so the audience won't ruin the whole performance by yelling for the Maytals' most famous song. Newer songs like "In the Dark," "Funky Kingston," and the great "Time Tough" alternate with uncanny Redding impersonations and a fey reggae version of John Denver's "Country Roads." But where Denver drowns his pretty song in gooey syrup, Toots gooses it with rhythm and gives it a new life it probably didn't know it had. Toots's newer songs reflect

his growing preoccupation with Rasta themes ("Living in the Ghetto," "Rasta Man") tempered with the essential kindness and humanity that have always characterized his music. A new song, "Premature," advises the would-be Jamaican lecher to "Send the girl back home/Send that girl back home/She's underage." Toots is apparently concerned for the in-

creasing number of female children producing babies in Jamaica these days. He claims to have sired twelve of his own with an undetermined number of women.

While we were in Jamaica, Toots and the Maytals were on the road in Europe with one of the better reggae ensembles, guitarist Hux Brown's group, the Dynamites (Paul Douglas on drums, bassist Jackie Jackson, and veteran session keyboardist Winston Wright). In Jamaica we occasionally traveled with a representative of Island Records, and everywhere we went reggae musicians would earnestly inquire about the Maytals' progress, how were they received, what were the audiences like, is the music making it out there? If hope and thought-force alone propelled the spread of reggae, Dread music would now be bubbling under the hot hundred on Neptune.

We finally caught up with Toots months later, still touring effortlessly, in a motel room on an expressway south of San Francisco. We knocked on his door. No answer. We pushed the door and found it ajar. In the bed a formless shape lay completely under the covers. We cleared our throats. It was four in the afternoon. The figure rolled over and stretched. Then a head surfaced and regarded us, heavily lidded. "Good thing you come," it said blearily. "Me was having a dream that a mon was shootin' me in the stomach again and again."

We asked, "Did it hurt?"

"It hurt bad but he couldn't kill me. I wouldn't die for that ras clot . . . good thing you came when you did. Give a minute to get I-self smooth and we eat."

Toots swung his legs over the side of the bed, dressed only in his shorts, and popped a button on his cassette player. Out came a rapid croaking prayer followed by an old Methodist hymn with the words modified slightly for Rasta theology. Over the chanters the high harmony of Toots's powerful voice was clear, almost overbearing. Then the monotone croaking commenced again. "We call that daily praise. We do this every day at home. I record it on this little thing and tek it with me around the world. It give me the strength I need. That, and this." He reached into a white envelope and pulled out a few pungent ganja buds. He rolled them into a spliff—buds, seeds, stems, everything combustible—lit it, and smoked as he put on his reggae zoot suit for the night's show.

"I invented reggae. Wrote a song called 'Do the Reggay' in 196—I don't remember when it was, but I wrote it anyway. It's true. Reggae just mean comin' from the people. Everyday t'ing, like from the ghetto. So all of our music, our Jamaican rhythm, comin' from the major-

Toots at home

The Maytals rehearse

ity. Everyday t'ing that people use like food; we just put music to it and mek a dance out of it, y'know. I would say that reggae come from the roots of the reggae that is the ghetto. When you say reggae you mean *regular,* majority. And when you say reggae it mean poverty, suffering, Rastafari, everything. Ghetto. It's music from the rebels, people who don't have what they want.

"I'm a Rastaman. I'm a *Rastafari.* You have many kind of men who's Rastafari. You have *natty,* and you have Rastaman. A lot of people really don't understand. A man cannot *turn* Rasta. He has to do the thing that God would do, only then he become a Rastaman. Because God is Rasta. Rastaman don't do

nothing that is wrong, and him have love for each and every one. God makes us of hisself. God is not far out. He's a peaceful, loving man. That's why my songs and my lyrics and my record sound like this. Cause I'm a religious, *true-born* Rastaman. A prophet, y'know? With my singing I prophesy t'ings. I sing about reality, t'ings that can happen, *real* t'ings.

"Musicians do the work of God. Really. Not when they sing about some girl in the bed, but when they sing about something that come from way down here, something that's real, Godliness, uprightness, loving kindness. Y'know? Then he becomes prophet of God.

"I no Locksman. I trim my hair, got it all

combly and nice. We got to try to be like God. You do the work of God, you become God. Do the work of Satan 'and you become Satan. He's in us and will always be in us. So I represent God, and God is Man. I serve him in freedom and truth. I go to the place at home where we assemble and we praise God daily. 'Cause the word is God. We read our Bible and we chant our chant, the brethren together, and we *feel* it. That the way we get blessed from God, y'know?

"I was very small and felt I would like to be a prophet when I was a boy. Sometime I would start to sing and the song would break my heart, y'know? I'd feel so *glorious,* y'know, so *good.* I knew I could be something special

when I was singing in Sunday school. Now, y'know, my heart is my church and I'm feeling the way I used to feel when I was a boy every day. As for dis herb here . . . well, *herb is the healing of the nation; it was written from creation!*"

Conventional wisdom has constructed a reggae triumvirate that doesn't exist—Marley, Toots, Cliff. All are master musicians; these are the three who have been heavily publicized outside of Jamaica. But when the Jamaican is discussing the music he might mention a singer named Bob Andy in the same breath with Bob Marley, pass over Toots as a parvenue Rasta, and claim not to have heard any-

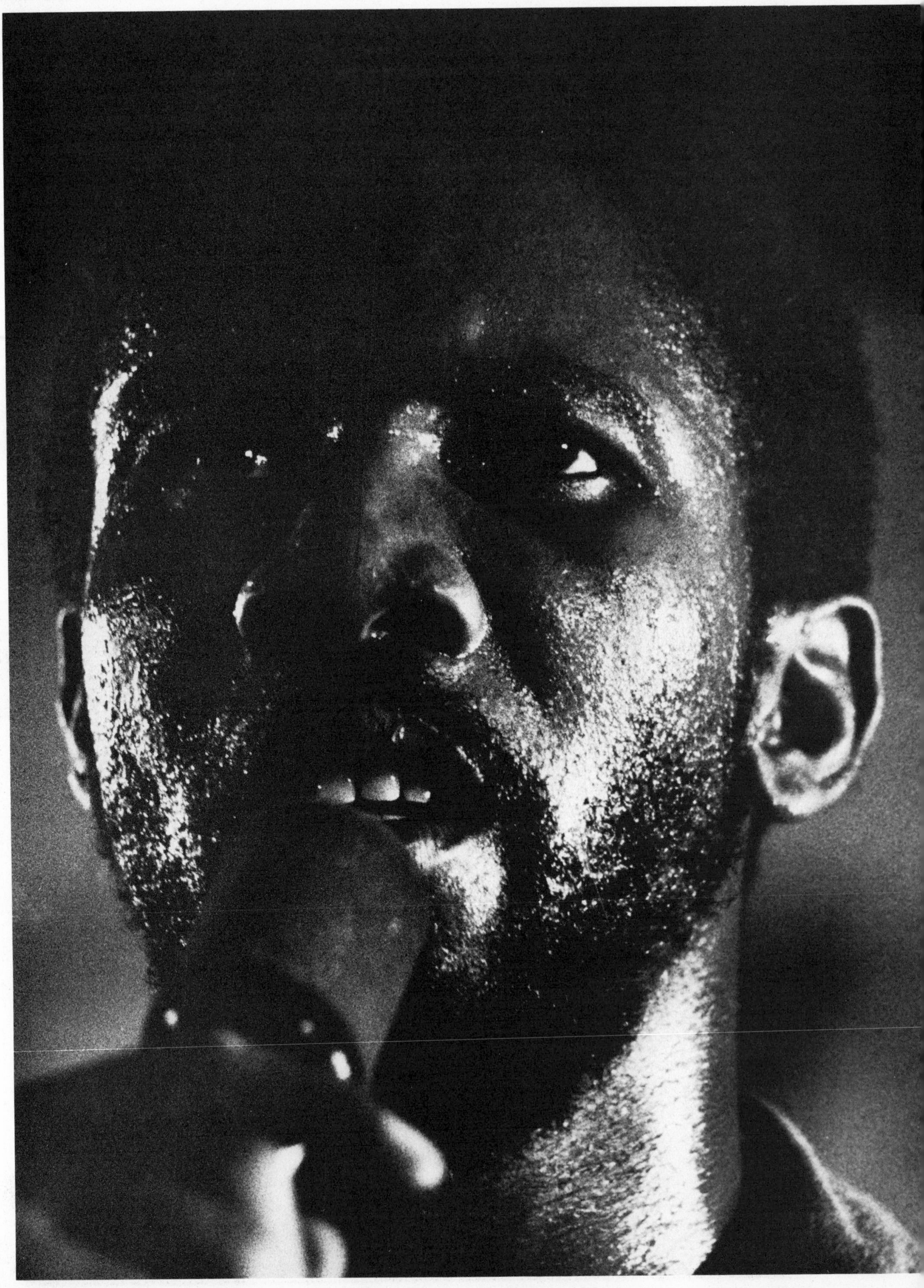

Joe Higgs

thing of Cliff in a few years. Ask the average foreign reggae fan who he respects and you'll get told Marley. Ask Marley and you'll get Big Youth. Ask Big Youth and you'll get Marley and John Coltrane. Ask most reggae musicians who they respect and almost invariably you'll get told Joe Higgs.

The unsung Joe Higgs is often ranked with Bob Marley as one of the greatest singers Jamaica has produced, and clearly is reggae's major theoretician. Describing himself usually as a protest singer, Higgs has an unadorned style not unlike that of the old Jamaican country singers. His hits include "The World Is Upside Down," "Fire Burning," "Don't Mind Me," and "Wave of War." In the early '60s, Higgs teamed with his Trench Town neighbor Delroy Wilson to form a successful duo recording Jamaican "blues" for West Indian Records, an old-line label then owned by Edward Seaga, currently the leader of the opposi-

tion Jamaica Labor Party. Seaga left the record business to go into politics (a completely logical shift) during the height of Higgs & Wilson's fame, and the pair went through several more producers before splitting in 1964.

It's well known in Jamaica that Joe Higgs was the musical force behind the early Wailers, having organized the band, taught them timing, tactics, harmony, breathing, *duende,* and sound precision. But Higgs has usually been and continues to be a shadow figure for the younger reggae stars. His disdain of commerciality has kept him out of the spotlight and relegated him to a supporting role, where perhaps he does his best work. Higgs toured America with the Wailers in 1974, replacing Bunny Livingston on hand drums and high harmony. Currently he tours with Jimmy Cliff, acting as supporting act, compere, second voice, and bandleader. When working with Cliff, Higgs is always dressed in full fatigue uniform behind his timbales, shouting and peppering at Cliff's band to get them hot. He might sing his 1970 hit "Fire Burning" or another of his songs. After Cliff comes out Higgs does a gentle fade into the band and people tend to stop seeing him. But as much as anyone else, Higgs is one of the reasons that Jamaican music is making its way in the world.

We first found Joe Higgs at Jimmy Cliff's house with his big momma, a woman named Dahlia, who was "lookin' after" Joe and evidently taking real good care of him. We met later at talent agent Tommy Cowon's hangout-headquarters on Oxford Street. From the outset Higgs said he didn't want to talk about anything but music:

"I was born in the poorer part of Kingston and was raised in Trench Town and then spent the better part of ten years there. It was *always* very violent as it is now, the way any ghetto is violent, a place of competition and survival. Let them say what they want, but nothing has changed for the smaller man in Jamaica.

"Gradually I found that music was part of me. Used to play like drums, y'know? A little guitar. I guess you could say I'm a part of the reggae tradition, one of the originators of the music, y'know wha I mean? I change whole reggae concept from time to time. For example there was a time one song of mine change the whole pace of the music, 'How Can I Be Sure.' Was a very good song.

"I start recording in 1960, but it was a different sound then, a time of ska, more to the African touch, consciously or uncon-

Joe Higgs and Jimmy Cliff

sciously, more relevant to the drums. Protest and confrontation—this is the context that reggae come from. The nearest thing to reggae for spirit would be jazz, modern jazz. You put out what you feel and amalgamate a song by virtue of unity.

"I don't mix music with my creed like some. For me they are two different things. Every man call upon God his own way. Truth and rights, regardless of race and creed. That's what I'm defending now. Reggae a music of power! Reggae meant to change the system! As long as they buy reggae in the States and England, we all right! Ha-ha!

"I don't talk about politics. A man's political beliefs are his own. Jamaica's a place of confrontation. Doesn't pay to talk.

"The Wailers? Well . . . I'm the creator. I'm the one who really mold the Wailers as a group. I taught them harmony step by step. I taught them to keep a straight line in harmony, taught them techniques and craft. Craft is something you have to apply to your voice when you are not fit enough to sing. Bob Marley was influenced by my works, but I'm not prepared to say that. I am not proud of being Bob Marley's teacher, I'm proud of being Joe Higgs. I have my part to play. But last year I spent six months in Los Angeles and Marley billboard on Sunset Strip all the time. So, if you spend the money, you get famous.

"Ras *clot*—the obstacles of life! I've never found an honest producer, so I'm always on the run. The musicians here do have a union, but a reggae musician has no understanding of international agreements. Much foolishness. Much confusion. Reggae musicians don't even play in the North Coast hotels for the well-heeled people because they look for the kind of guy who has a neat appearance that won't scare the tourists and won't smoke pot around the place. Most reggae musicians not like dot, Ras. . . .

"As for Jimmy Cliff . . . Cliff a very very

Junior Byles (a reggae legend) with Joe Higgs

very unselfish person. Not like the rest of them. We are different creeds but that makes no difference. That's why we don't discuss it. I'm a Rastaman who don't preach.

"Why do we always wear army clothes? Because we fight here every day. I love the soldier so I wear his clothes. It means, *get involved*. The soldier and the musician are tools for change. That is why we were created."

Big Youth

The Rockers
Meet Dub
Reggae Uptown

It's easier for camel to pass through needle's eye
Than for version to die.

I Roy

In the early days you couldn't hear Jamaican music on Jamaican radio. There was only one station, the Jamaican Broadcasting Corporation, run by the government and modeled on the BBC, and it would no more play ska, rock-steady, or slum reggae than it would Little Richard or Fats Domino. The only way Jamaicans heard music they wanted to dance to was on the traveling sound systems that sprang up in the early and mid-'50s. To attract a loyal following, the sound systems relied not only on the freshness of their records but on the microphone talents of the sound-system operator or his surrogate disc jockey, talking over the record being played, goosing the dancers and getting their spirits up with hip commentary, squawks, updated nursery phrases and demented vocal riffs. The sound-system bosses like Coxone Dodd and Prince Buster went on to rule the Jamaican recording industry for a time. Others, like the late Duke Reid, were the pioneers of hipness and unadulterated flash that started a subschool of reggae called variously dub music, version, or deejay records.

Of all the old sound-system men, Duke Reid was the most outrageous. He'd show up for a dance wearing a gilt crown and an ermine-fringed jacket, a pair of Colt .45s in twin holsters, a shotgun strapped to his back, and his chest crossed by cartridge belts. On his feet were hand-tooled Texas boots. The effect was something like a Wild West pirate terminally wasted on white rum and too much ganja.

That was only the Duke's *look*. When he got up and started deejaying over the music, punctuating and mocking the records with banter and shrieks—*Waauugh! Good Gawd Amighty! Ow!Ow!Ow!Ow!Ow!Ow! Have Mercy!*—the dancers' tenuous connections with reality tended to snap like electric guitar strings turned ten octaves too tight.

Eventually this vocal deejaying was augmented by messing with the tone knobs and echo and reverb switches, often rendering a well-known tune unrecognizable and creating a new hybrid in the process. This was the beginning of the beast called "dub."

Jamaican engineer King Tubby used to mix Sir Coxone's two-track tapes with musicians on one track and vocals on the other. He would then make an acetate on the final mix, but to test the quality of the voices, Tubby would drop out the music track for a chorus.

He explains that it got to be real exciting when the music dropped back in. He took five or so of these acetates to a Coxone dance one night and the crowd wouldn't let him play anything else. Later producer Bunny Lee began to back all his singles with a "version," souping up the sound (after Tubby's example) with great puddles of echo and reverb.

Most of the old sound-system men are still around Kingston, trying to survive through the days of political unrest, slow record sales, and a temporary ban on dances. King Tubby sits in his shop repairing amplifiers, putting on his trademark crown when visitors arrive. Bunny Lee is producing records but his shop is closed and no one knows where he is. Sir Coxone—Clement Dodd—hasn't been seen lately either, and there's talk he's moved to England for good.

King Tubby

Big Youth

Prince Buster

One day Jimmy Cliff took us over to Prince Buster's record shop to check out one of the most successful of the old sound-system men. Buster played a deejay in *The Harder They Come* who introduces Ivan's song by playing it at a dance. A trained boxer who fought under a phony name, Buster is one of the heavies from the ska days, and now he lives in tony Beverly Hills way above Kingston. We talked to him in a little room in back of his shop:

"I was named *Busta,* after Bustamante [the Jamaican union boss, Labor prime minister, and national hero] because there was political violence when I was born and my mother almost got killed on her way to maternity. Later I change the spelling to Buster. After I was a

boxer, a Floyd Patterson peekaboo type of fighter, I went to work as the record genius for Coxone's system. When a hit American song come on a 78 in those days, one would immediately scratch the label off so no one else could get it and no one know what it is 'cept the deejay. Like T-Bone Walker, B.B. King, Gene Phillips. There was no radio in those days and sound system was everything. To hear a new record thousands would go to the dances."

Buster says he was a victim of financial injustice as a deejay and had to go out on his own. He borrowed money and opened what he claims was the first record shop in Kingston. Then he started making records himself: "Little Honey" in 1956, and later "They Got to

The legendary U Roy

Go," which protested the supremacy of the big sound systems. "I told them they had to go and make way for the new local music, which was ska. I was the first promoter of ska in Jamaica. My sound system was based on ska and that's why I came on number one. What people don't know is there never really was a dance called ska." [Cliff: "It was just a bunch of businessmen coming together to exploit it. Ska was never a dance, just music."]

Buster continued, "The proper dance in Jamaica to ska music was the bebop dance, push and spin, and natural Jamaican things like flashing [snapping] the fingers and pickup moves from Pocomania and mento. All of reggae music is still basically ska. The strongest sellers still have that good afterbeat." Buster went on to make huge hits out of lewd parodies like "Wreck a Poom Poom" (to the tune of "Little Drummer Boy") and "Judge Dread," in which he sentenced the Rude Boys to four hundred years on general principles.

Now he's waiting it out like so many Jamaicans, hoping the political turmoil will end and life can return to some semblance of normality. "Yes, the violence has killed the dances," he says. "If I gave a dance now the people would be slaughtered. I say, leave the people with the guns alone. The politicians should be brought to trial."

In 1970 a deejay calling himself U Roy popularized the talk-over record and reggae hasn't been the same since. Working as a deejay for King Tubby's system in the late '60s, U Roy (Ewart Beckford), from Jones Town, drew on the crazy ravings of another deejay named King Stitt to produce a maniacal, screaming, soul-baring presence that energized any party and turned the dancers into jelly. When U Roy raved it sounded like a hundred severely ruptured parrots. Undoubtedly fed up with having his improvisational flights of Dread brilliance evanesce like so much tropic breeze every night, U Roy decided to

capture them permanently. He took a reggae song, tuned out the vocal track, and dubbed in his own commentary, jokes, and shamanic bleats. At one time in late 1970 he had three talk-over songs in the Jamaican Top Ten (this was before the charts were banned): "Wear You to the Ball," "Rule the Nation," and "Wake the Town." Later he came up with monsters like "Flashing My Whip," "Love I Tender," and "Your Ace from Space." U Roy was such a culture hero to Jamaicans and immigrant West Indians that dozens of copycats sprang up overnight despite U Roy's piteous admonition "Do not imitate, because I originate."

U Roy might have been the first, but now dub music is ubiquitous and currently the most popular form of reggae in Jamaica. Every Jamaican single now released has a

U Roy at work

remixed version of the original on the flip side without the vocals, enabling the deejay to "skank" or "toast" over the single, or for the "version" to be used by a deejay as the basis for a new composition of his own, after some cash has changed hands between the two producers. The musicians or authors of the version never get paid if the song is covered by anybody else. About the only thing the Jamaican musicians' union has been able to do is get deejay records banned from both radio stations, a no-win decision that doesn't help anyone since dub albums by such as King Tubby and the Upsetters outsell everything else, including the Wailers.

After two years as the king of the deejays U Roy went to London to work for a spell and then returned to Jamaica and retired, having run out of smoke and depressed at the talented imitators who were taking over his thing. In 1975 he emerged from his hiatus like a triumphant grand master to record an album called *Dread in a Babylon*. The next year he actually toured Europe and the States. Opening for the Mighty Diamonds and the Maytals, U Roy would come onstage in an orange cape and go through three songs in as many minutes before disappearing again, oblivious to any cries for more. He would run backstage, take off his cape and performing clothes, check his locks in the mirror, light a spliff, and change into a black velvet suit and a purple velvet pimp's hat. On his right wrist he wore a huge gold bracelet engraved with "U ROY." A small and very gentle man whose fierce eyes belie his sweet nature, he would tell you that his favorite song was his own "Chalice in the Palace," which postulates a ganja session with Elizabeth II. Few of the young reggae fans who came out those nights to see Toots realized they were witnessing the comeback of a legend, and usually let U Roy go without calling for an encore.

U Roy's imitators were legion, but only a handful were any good. I Roy, an accountant from Spanish Town, was one of the earliest and one of the best. After U Roy faded, I Roy was the top deejay in Jamaica until the recent emergence of Big Youth. I Roy, widely accused of stealing everything from U Roy including most of his name, was actually a brilliant original, with a big reverb boom and an utterly penetrating shriek that could turn the brains into boiled ackee. I Roy was really Roy Reid, with a better claim to the name than the original. I Roy was also even *goofier* than U Roy, spicing his cracked riffs with street games, idiotic ramblings, cheap doggerel, and nursery phrases. His favorite protagonist is Goosey Gander. He is known for such Jamaican hits as "Natty Down Deh," "Welding," "Dread in the West," "Teapot," and "The Black Bullet." But I Roy is also known for his comic savagery, as demonstrated on the great series of feud records exchanged by I Roy and another famous dub deejay, Prince Jazzbo. It started when I Roy released, out of the blue, a single called "Straight to Jazzbo's Head," which taunted: "Jazzbo if you were a jukebox, I wouldn't put a dime into your slot," and "Russian roulette blood clot on ya . . ." This kind of talk can be an occasion for whipping out the ratchet knives for a little carving, but the clearly dismayed Prince Jazzbo instead issued a rejoinder: "Straight to I Roy's Head," a single that ran: "Hail Jazzbo-ites! I Roy you a *bwoy*—move out de way—cause you imitate the great U Roy. I Roy you a bwoy! How come trouble Prince Jazzbo? Prince Jazzbo never trouble you," and on and on like that, Jazzbo all the time tearful and almost sobbing and breaking down.

I Roy, with antarctic cool, struck back at the Prince with the devastating "Sit Down Yourself Jazzbo," which began with a little playlet:

POLICE: Good morning. I have a summons here for Prince, uh, Princess Jazzbo from Alligator Pond, Crocodile Avenue. Do any of you

Prince Jazzbo

Dillinger

Dread know him?

DREAD: Yes Roots! She live in the window of an oil shop.

OLD CRONE: Jazzbo! Jazzbo! Babylon a come!

POLICE: (pounding on door) Jazzbo! Jazzbo!

Wake up Wake up!! Look like we have fe kick down the door.

(Heavy crashing noise)

CRONE: HEEhee Jazzbo! Babylon a come! Heeheeheeheeheehee. . . .

This fades into a supersuave I Roy telling Jazzbo to sit down and pull himself together, throwing in a sneer of homosexual references ("Jazzbo you bound to get flop/If you go fe MoBay and sit on a lap") and several more gratuitous comments as well: "Jazzbo when you sneeze/you remind me of the Japanese/ You teeth full of cheese."

The I Roy-Prince Jazzbo feud was eagerly consumed by Jamaican fans and made money for both deejays. I Roy kept sneaking insidious Jazzbo jabs into new songs until Jazzbo became a ridiculous figure and his career as a reggae madman was somewhat in eclipse.

Another dub master is the highly respected Dennis Alcapone, who began with "Ripe Cherry," built on Eric Donaldson's 1972 "Cherry Oh Baby." A Dread deejay called Dillinger also has become popular on the strength of the enormous single, "CB 200," which celebrates *in extremis* the Jamaican religious cult of the Honda motorbike.

The hands-down current champion of deejaying and dub reggae is a conscientious Dreadlock named Manley Buchanen, a former Kingston cabbie who goes by the name Big Youth. Big Youth is the reggae future, representing a bigger sound, more bass, heavier drums—in Jamaica that's the avant-garde. Big Youth is so popular he's been called a human *Gleaner*. Meaning that his records are the only way a significant number of Jamaicans find out what's happening in the world at large. Big Youth started out as a common deejay with a motorbike single, "Ace 90 Skank." His two singles dealing with the 1973 heavyweight boxing championship match held in Kingston —"George Foreman" and "Foreman and Frazier"—gained him fame, since the Jamaican favorite, Foreman, knocked out Frazier easily. "House of Dreadlocks" and "Natty Cultural Dread" established Big Youth as a voice of Rastafarianism, and now even Bob Marley says that Big Youth is his favorite reggae musician. During our stay in Jamaica, Big Youth's latest single, "Hit the Road Jack!" (which has a gonzo segue in and out of "What the World Needs Now"), was number one on all the illegitimate record shop charts and was the only thing resembling a deejay record being played on the radio. People either love Big Youth or hate him with a passion. He has lately tried to transcend his deejay past by recording original singles of his own. The first ones are selling like mad and Big Youth is riding high, the hippest and Dreadest reggae cat around anywhere.

We found Big Youth's house in a middle-class neighborhood in Kingston. His yard was filled with motorcycles and dozens of Rastas smoking and testifying to each other. Trying to cleverly sync into Jamaican time patterns, we arrived an hour after we were expected, hoping this way to be on time. Actually, we had miscalculated. We waited another hour and a half for Big Youth, who didn't get home until sunset. During this time heavy-looking Rastas came and went on motorbikes. The

Coxson Dodd

scene was a hangout on the order of Bob Marley's place, only the Dreads seemed to be younger. It was a different generation. Big Youth finally arrived flashing his locks and the heart-shaped golden caps on his teeth. He's young, aggressive, and congenial. He took us into his parlor to tape a conversation under a bare bulb. On an old table was a tiny cassette machine connected to a pair of tinny speakers. Pictures of Haile Selassie on the walls. Motorcycle magazines carpeted the floor. He played us the demos of some singles—"Ten Against One," "Stand Up for Your Rights," and "Jim Screechee," which had the line "John Coltrane died in vain of Love Supreme."

After telling a couple of noisy Dreads outside to shut up, Big Youth began to articulate his story:

"I was born in Trench Town, at the Victoria Jubilee. That's the main place where most children are born in Kingston. So I would say I have had the *privilege* of growing up in Trench Town and all the other ghetto towns. It's all just one town anyway. I used to be a music lover just like anybody else, y'know, the type of people we grew up with in the ghetto is the kind of people who say *yes* to music, right? I used to be a regular dance fan and always exercised myself at the mike every time I get the privilege. I would sing or rap along with it. Coming along now in the late '60s come a man called U Roy, right? And he was inspirable to me anyway. I like what he was doing and always think I can do it. There was one dance I remember: things go wrong, the music mislead, the right deejay didn't turn up and I get the right and privilege to express I-self, and people have a good night. Soon I go into studio and do this song—'Man if you come from afar in a bus or a car you should make love not war . . .' That song only sell a few copies and I got twenty dollars for it. I didn't even think it was worthwhile trying anymore, but I did a song called 'Black Cinderella'—they call it 'Black Cindy.' My songs were fascinating—I *knew* it—but nothin' was comin' my way. You know how the artists was getting ripped off by the producer down here, *every* producer, not partial. None of the man that sing get good treatment whatsoever from them. Well, I was doing 'Black Cindy' and dying to hear I-self on the radio. I did one called 'Tell It Black' but it still wasn't a big thing. But in the ghetto where the lively people are, they're moving to my music so I am encouraged, y'know wha I mean?

"Then I do one called 'When Revolution Come'; this was for Prince Buster. It be number one on all the charts, number one for JBC, number one for RJR. And until this day I mon still get no royalties from Prince Buster. I confront him but I been strick down with guns! If you are a Rastaman, nobody want to respect you. He call hisself a Muslim! *Ras clot!*

"My big hit was 'Ace Go Skank.' That was one relating to bikes again: 'If ya ride like lightning, ya crash like thunder . . .' Then from there it was one called 'Screaming Target,' 'The Killer,' 'Tea for Two,' 'Rocking,' 'Cool Breeze,' 'Dock of the Bay.' There were times on the charts when I would have five records in the Top Ten.

"I claim the popularity of being the number-one man through all these times. Only Dennis Brown could stand with Big Youth. But all that fame and fancy producers didn't make me *nothing*. Some of this music make me famous in England even though I never been there. *But I will not fight for money.* [He kisses his teeth bitterly.] These producers are not so-called thieves, they are direct thieves, who rape and rob you. I mon see no good in none of them. So a man like I, I try and produce I songs I-self. I can do it because I have an impact on the people. Ya dig? Every show that Big Youth attends—Blood *clot!* I do it every time. Big Youth has a flock!

"Now I think there is a conspiracy out to get I. The whole thing about music is that with the right promotion of the right song at the right time, it ain't no problem. I mon don't think reggae is different from any other music. I think it's the same as jazz, with the same feeling as jazz. Some of these lyrics related to a people and their environment, but that does not mean that people living in other environments won't be able to understand them. I whole relation is to reality. God of all relation is reality. Ya dig?"

What do you think of the other reggae musicians?

"Well, I mon think that Jimmy Cliff is a nice film star. But I mon not fascinated by Jimmy Cliff's kind of reggae. Right? Toots? Toots now have a Negro spiritual style, an African kind of thing with jumpin' and revivin' and spirits, y'know? I mon like Toots himself as a performer but . . . I mon love Roots Marley. I mon believe in Roots Marley ten thousand times. See it? Roots Marley draw one a all dem names men call. It's not from partiality because him a Dreadlocks but because him telling people the truth. Mon see it? I mon say 'natty dread' before Bob. I mon was the first that seh 'natty dread in a Babylon.' They make it like Bob was the first mon to say it but it was my original. Yes Rasta! I mon love Bob, but I mon *love* Big Youth."

Why is Big Youth called a human Gleaner?

"Well, I mon sing about the truth and the rights. Try to portray to the people that the way of harmony is to share with each other. Nothing makes one man different from another man. We try in our music to unite the people that everybody live together. No more songs about girls . . ."

How did reggae evolve in Trench Town?

"In Jamaica, in the world, you have races and classes. Some people think they are better than some, some people think they are on top. We have the haves and the have-nots. Trench Town is a place they built up out of shacks, y'know? That is not to say that the people who come from Trench Town are not educated. They are the great Jamaican people. They are the people who must face reality. They are hungry and suffering, yeah mon. And it is so sad and unnecessary. I mean, you don't have fe see people on the *ground*. Some of them fall that them have nothin' fe eat and all dem things. *Ras clot!* Those are the people that have to face reality. Ya have places like Jones Town and Rose Town and another nearby called Hose Town and these are complicated places—it's not different from tribes, from tribes living in Africa, and out of this comes the feeling of reggae."

What's going on in Jamaica now?

"Not only Jamaica, mon. Look at Africa. Look at Vietnam. Jamaica is run on the idea

Big Youth does a wheelie

that some people kyaan afford to send their children to school. That makes some people very mad. If you don't have literacy people is hungry and don't have peace of mind, right? A mon kyaan live clean. [Sucks his teeth violently.] Listen, Trench Town is no different from anyplace else. Violence comes like tribal war. Youths who cannot stand inflation and confusion kill each other. It looks like political violence, but it's not. Ahh, the whole Trench Town system put the fear on people, but now they start to revolute and think about their rights. It's the prophecy, y'unnerstand?"

Big Youth seems to be the chief of the Kingston motorbike cult. . . .

"But I mon think that bike is dangerous. I think car is dangerous but bike is dangerous more. But it's not every man that can afford to buy a car in Jamaica so we know more about bikes. [Big Youth laboriously fills a chalice with ganja and a little tobacco and stokes up a good cloud, vanishing for a moment.] Me was looking for a point here. . . ."

You were talking about bikes.

"If you're a Dread and you're riding a bike nobody want respect you and like that. That is where part of my revolution is comin' in. The Dread who sees the truth and the rights and the reality and the injustice is the new kind of Christian. He is in front of the world religions. Everything the Dreadlocks try to do is fought by Babylon. Babylon is wicked and ignorant and sick people. Me think me supposed to be free but if Dread I'm not! These Dreadlocks are my prison bars in Babylon. They send people to fight us, sick police. I mon people are the last class, and are seeking truth and rights. Rasta know the truth—the youths are the generation of them that see the Father's face. This generation not stand for no nonsense no more. Babylon is a society built up out of slavery and segregation, right? Pope Paul is an evil form; he is the head of Babylon. He control the Queen and set up the slavery. If I mon could get hold of the Pope I would . . . ."

What is your vision of the future of reggae?

"Well, reggae become international. If biased people give a listen, I mon think reggae become the new music, right? Took people time to understand John Coltrane. Same with reggae, ya dig? With the right promotion, I and I brethren can do it. I mon Big Youth ready for tour and the right exposure. I mon think America is the place that need it. When the time come, *Big Youth explode America. . . .*"

The Heptones at play

The
Third World
Nashville

come midnight, the dance get foggy and daughter dance
to the heavy throb of
the rhythm, the strong smell of grass and soon the music
begin to penetrate everybody

—Leroy Sibbles (of the Heptones)

Third World Nashville. That's what they're calling funky Kingston these days. The Nashville of the Caribbean. It's a boom town—fifteen studios and seventy-five independent producers and hundreds of singers and players that'll work for a little smoke and the hell of it. And all the slick carpetbaggers flying in these days from the Babylonian music cartels in New York and Los Angeles now that Marley is on the charts and rumors of all these other bucolic geniuses are floating around. And it's true. Even though times might be a little slow due to the pressure, it's still pretty busy—thirty new singles launched like trench mortars into the Kingston marketplace every week. With a population of about two million

that means the reggae industry has the highest per capita singles release in the world.

But Kingston is more like Nashville without any of Nashville's tenuous guarantees. The Jamaican reggae industry is like the American music industry without the lawyers. Contracts are nonexistent; rip-offs, bribery, and intra-industry violence are the rules of the game. Official record charts from Stations JBC and RJR have been banned since late 1974, when payola started to get out of hand and deejays on the two stations were threatened by gunmen if certain songs weren't played. According to veteran reggae talent agent Tommy Cowon: "At one point in the days of the charts it got so bad that a producer who had a

Federal Records, Kingston

number-eight song would kill to get it to number one if that would help him any." These days the only reliable charts are those published by the larger record shops on the basis of sales and requests. Dub music is banned on the radio because the British program director of the JBC decided that, since the musicians only get paid for recording the A side of the single, if the B-side dub version is used by another artist, the original musicians will have been cheated. There is of course something to that point of view, but as Cowon comments, "The problem is that many people don't care for the vocal track on the A side but love the rhythm of the dub on the B side. And we keep tellin' them—how can reggae expand into the world if it is banned at home?"

But walk into Randy's Record Mart on the North Parade in downtown Kingston and you'll find things are hot. The clerks take turns

deejaying, pushing knobs rendering the latest singles into molten blobs of bass and echo. Ask to hear something from Randy's custom charts and you'll get ten seconds of reggae shard before the needle lifts again and you have to decide whether you want the thing or not. Ask a clerk for the new one by the Slickers and he'll say they just ran out. Ask the next clerk for the new one by the Slickers and he'll produce a mint copy from a stack of fifty behind the counter. Buying records in Jamaican shops is a matter of persistence and who you know.

Randy's chart is the most accurate barometer of what Jamaicans—the planet's most discriminating reggae audience—are listening to. Big Youth and the Mighty Diamonds usually seem to occupy the first two positions, followed by maybe Bob Marley, or Max Romeo, or Jacob Miller. Popular, "society" and commercial singers like Pluto Shervington, Jackie

Singles

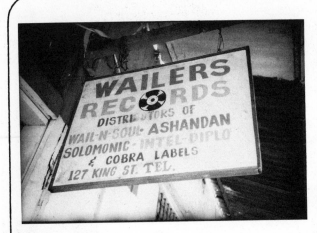

Brown, Jonnie Clarke, John Holt, Bob Andy, and Horace Andy usually have strong singles as well. Dillinger is the hottest deejay currently if the chart is trustworthy. The chart also points to reggae's essential role of journalism in Jamaica. One chart published during the 1976 Angolan Revolution (tacitly supported by the Jamaican Government) listed three related singles ("Angola," "M.P.L.A.," and "Let Go Violence"), all by one militant group, the Revolutionaires. On the day we arrived in Jamaica a mysterious shipment of poisoned counter flour went out to country stores and several dozen people died after eating contaminated bread. Within *one week* of this incident three flour singles had made the charts: "Killer Flour," by Jah Lloyd; "Poison Flòur," by Doctor Alimantado; and the torrential "Flour Power," by a demon named Naggo Morris, a ghoulish tape-splice riff laced with obscene funk and macabre litanies: "Flour kill the auntie, flour kill the uncle, flour kill the nephew . . . its a *killer.*"

Justice can be served in oblique ways. In Jamaican pop culture the reggae producer has become a standard stereotype caricature for greed, cunning, and villainy. In all our travels in search of reggae we did not meet one musician who thought he was receiving what he was owed by his producer. In *The Harder*

They Come, Mr. Hilton, the dishonest, manipulative producer, was the blackest hat. A typical reggae producer is a stock comic figure on the lively Kingston stage. A new play, *The Quickie,* by Stafford Harrison, casts a producer as an obstacle that a young Jamaican must overcome in his confusion over Rasta versus bourgeois values.

One morning we stopped in at Harry J's studio on Roosevelt Road. Harry Johnson might be called a prototypical reggae producer except that he's done much better than most. He has his own studio (where most of the Wailers' material is recorded) and production company and drives a rust-gold Grand Prix. We were hoping to cull some information from Harry on reggae economics, but we made the mistake of bringing him the English pressing of a new Island Records single by one

Doctor Alimantado   "Dread flash him locks anna weak heart drop."

Harry J

of his acts, the Heptones. We thought this might give Harry a charge but again we figured wrong. Production credit on the single was given to the engineer who recorded the session, and not Harry J. To put it mildly, Harry J was pissed off. "Dis, dis dis . . . *dis a bumba clot!*" he kept stammering over and over again. Harry J stormed through the premises, waved the single like a dead baby, and appeared grief-stricken. He crashed through the studio door, interrupting a Jackie Brown session in progress, shouting, "Dis a real bumba clot!" He ran around in a state for fifteen minutes, bugging the secretaries and even rapping out the sad story in thick patois for a couple of wasted loiterers who were hanging out in back.

Later, pacified somehow, Harry J sat at his desk and talked for a moment. "Always had a band from school days, called the Virtues. After a while I start managing the band, get-

ting into the business sector. The band broke up for financial reasons and I started selling insurance. But still always kept in contact with artists and musicians." Harry claims his first single as a producer, "No More Heartaches," by the Beltones, sold fifty thousand copies in England without going on the charts. Then he hit with Lorna Bennet's classic, "Breakfast in Bed," a Nashville country and western tune that Harry thought would sound good as reggae. Now his stable includes Jackie Brown, the Heptones, Bob Andy (an important reggae belter), Marcia Griffiths (one of the Wailers' I-Threes and a haunting singer on her own), and the Cables, an offshoot of the Heptones.

The Heptones are Harry J's ackee and salt cod. The fundamental rock-steady trio has an American recording contract with Island Records, which pays all of Harry's production costs. On top of that, as producer, Harry takes

The Heptones-Leroy Sibbles (seated), Earl Morgan, Barry Llewellyn

Bunny Lee

25 per cent of the group's earnings. That's a lot.

The Heptones are Leroy Sibbles, Earl Morgan, and Barry Llewellen. Among the most melodic and the prettiest of the vocal trios, the Heptones are throwbacks to the halcyon days of rock-steady. The group formed in 1965 and had it's first hit the next year with the lewd "Fatty Fatty," which graphically explored the mystique of heavy women. Dozens of their classic singles were released in England by unscrupulous producers in the late '60s under various other names. They also recorded "Hippocrite" in 1971 and later such strong tunes as the hickbaiting "Country Boy" and the devastating "Mama Say." Their best song, "Book of Rules," captures the Heptones' lyric power, among the most complex and most direct in reggae:

Isn't it strange how princesses and
  kings
In clown-ragged capers in sawdust
  rings
While common people like you and
  me
We'll be builders for eternity
Each is given a bag of tools
A shapeless mask and a Book of rules

Harry J says, "There's a big gap between the commercial groups like the Wailers and the Maytals and the new young artists who are roots. The big boys use a different sound mix in different countries. A reggae song meant for the States will be mixed a little faster than one meant for Jamaica. The new boys have to be heavily promoted and there isn't enough money for that. They're barely surviving, some of them. We survive by giving the people what

The cricket pitch at Port Royal

they want to hear. We produce records that will sell in Jamaica."

Considering the frantic climate of the reggae industry in general, one tends to wonder why there isn't even more violence, and why the government doesn't step in to regulate now that reggae is supposed to surpass tourism and sugar as a major earner of foreign currency. A producer like Harry J survives in a market where one man produces, manufactures, distributes, promotes, and sometimes even retails his own records. Sometimes the blade takes the place of litigation. One sure way to identify a combat veteran of the reggae wars is the facial scars of a producer or musician. The worst kind of scar is known as the "telephone," an ear-to-throat cut that signifies

a settling of differences. Producer Bunny Lee. has one. If you look, you can see them all over town.

Almost fifty years after some forgotten jazz musicians recorded the first version of a song called "Black Star Line" in New York, a new song about Marcus Garvey's prophetic enterprise was shaking up the reggae scene in Jamaica. The singer called himself Fred Locks. His voice was an off-key yawp with a frightening edge to it, like a jagged piece of tin. His song "Black Star Liners" envisioned the fulfillment of Garvey's prophecy that seven miles of Black Star steamships would sail into Kingston Harbour someday to rescue the 140,000 chosen to escape from Babylon:

I can see them coming
I can see the Idrens running
I can hear the elders saying
These are the days for which we've
    been praying
Seven miles of Black Star Liners
Coming into the harbor . . .

You could hear that Fred Locks's voice was awful and weird, but it had an unnerving power. The song operated on so many levels of fantasy and reality that it both affirmed the Rasta belief in redemption and accentuated its ultimate futility. In the end, for the Rasta, suffering will prove enough. Suffering is his religion.

But how to find Fred Locks? He recorded the single with the young session leader Augustus Pablo, but Pablo was out of town. One day we ran into Alaric, one of the kif Dreads from Chela Bay, who was lounging in the shade of a tree in the yard of Micron, a record distributor and musicians' hangout on Retirement Road. Alaric gave us directions to his house in Harbour View and said that Fred would meet us there on Saturday.

That day we arrived an hour late in hope of being on time. No one answered the bell of the trim little tract house, so we drove a few more miles along the Palisadoes coast to Port Royal. For the latter half of the seventeenth century Port Royal was the pirate capital of the Caribbean, the free port where pirates and privateers sold captured Spanish and Portuguese booty to the British, working through the Sephardic middlemen who in their flight from the Spanish Inquisition had settled Jamaica before any other European colonists. Captain Henry Morgan and the "Brethren of the Coast" ruled Port Royal as the capital of a far-flung anarchist society that maintained most of the Caribbean under the black flag until 1692, when a massive earthquake dropped the whole town thirty feet below sea level and drowned most of the inhabitants. Of the old Port Royal, only its fortress and a few half-submerged buildings remain. But just like the old days, everyone in the surviving little village of Port Royal seems to be drunk on their feet.

Back in Harbour View we pull up to the house again and a tall red Dread beckons and walks over. He gets into the car. "I'm Fred," he says with a big smile. He's wearing a yellow cap and has blue eyes. He directs us to drive fast through the quiet streets until we reach another house. The neighborhood looks like a Los Angeles development circa 1955. Strictly Babylon. Shoes off at the doorstep. In the darkened living room, the World Book Encyclopedia and a stereo blaring calypso. Alaric is in the kitchen, presiding over an I-tal lunch; pots and pans of rice and greens whistle and

Fred Locks

hiss on the stove. The pungent aroma of Pickapeppa sauce. In the back Clarence is hanging up his laundry. Fred Locks walks into the yard and takes off his cap. As the wool tam comes off, Fred's pent-up locks start cascading over his shoulders like a lava flow, and the effect is startling and faintly erotic. It's called "flashing locks," and it's a popular Dread pastime.

Fred Locks speaks slowly and deliberately, carefully choosing his words. He first sang in obscure groups: the Lyrics, the Flames. Then "Black Star Liners" came together after two years of thinking about it. "Sometimes," he says, "names and titles sell the song more than the music. You have to pick apart the song to get the right title. That's why I took so long."

His real name is Stafford Elliot and he shed some light on the economics of a single. When he recorded the song he was paid $300 Jamaican. After 14,000 copies of "Black Star Liners" sold in Jamaica, Fred got a $1,000 advance for an English pressing. Fred doesn't know how well the song did in England, but in order for him to have gotten any royalties at all the song must have sold 10,000 copies to repay his advance at ten cents a copy sold. And Fred has been getting some royal-

ties, enough to put him in a little place in Harbour View. Fred Locks is thinking about moving to the States, and asks if his Rasta life would prevent him from coming. He says his father threw him out of the house in 1970 because of his locks. "I could already have my permanent visa in the States but for my Dreadlock life. All my aunties are in the Bronx and Brooklyn. My grandfather is in Harlem. Rasta means too much for me to leave." He sighs and snaps his braids out of his face. "About the States I don't know what fe think. Except my aim is to go up there and do enough work to come back and live down here."

Fred mentions his new single, an apocalyptic ditty called "The Last Days," which bodes of "rumors of war, and children having children." We ask how the record is doing and Fred says its okay but "I'm not really trustin' my producer. Sometime I have the feelin' him cheatin' me."

The tone of Dynamic Sound is all wrong for Kingston. Dynamic is Jamaica's premier recording studio and acts as a distributor of records for the entire Caribbean. Like its chief competitor, Federal Recording, Dynamic has its own printing and stamping machinery. A record can be recorded, mastered, stamped,

Byron Lee

take me into the studio, and I play on some of
the Wailers sessions with Lee Perry as producer. But every day I tried to get my own
music through to the producers. Every day I
walk up to them with a cassette machine, trying to get them to listen. And they laughed at
me and made a joke of me.

"One day I went to see a friend, and his girl
friend lend me this instrument, the melodica,
and I learn to play it and I go into the studio
and blow two tunes. One went to thirteen on
the charts and they give me this name,
Augustus Pablo. They tell me the name fit me
good."

With King Tubby at the controls Pablo has
made several best-selling dub albums, including *King Tubby Meets the Rockers Uptown*.
Like all dub, there are no vocals, just layers of
gritty funk turned inside out by studio tricks.
"We play reggae music by feeling it," Pablo
says. "We call it the 'Far East Sound' 'cause
we play in minor chords. Heh heh heh. When
you play those chords it's like a story without
words, and certain mon who go into deep
meditation can penetrate it. Some places no
check fe dub in Jamaica, just soul and disco.
But I couldn't turn against dub because I'm
part of it. I follow Selassie and dub music,
yeah mon!

"My ideal band? Well, I like to play with
Chinna Smith on lead guitar, Family Man on
bass. I penetrate every drummer's style.
Geoffrey Chung on keyboards. Bobby Ellis
and Tommy McCook on horns. That a reggae
band that would conquer the world."

Back at Tommy Cowon's yard we again ran
into Ras Michael, singer and head man of the
Sons of Negus. Ras Michael had a current hit,
"None A Jah Jah Children No Cry," and he
was bopping and twitching around the place
while Tosh played his acetates over and over
again. Michael's chief drummer and main
henchman, Kiddus, told us that the Sons of
Negus were the best band in Jamaica but

didn't play in public because of the Kingston
troubles. After consulting with Ras Michael,
he invited us to a Sons of Negus rehearsal the
next night. We gratefully accepted.

About the Mighty Diamonds:

The standard reggae grouping is the vocal
trio, as in the Maytals, the old Wailers, Burning Spear, the Prophets, the Heptones, and
dozens more. The newest and the youngest of
these trios is the Mighty Diamonds, composed
of Donald "Tabby" Sharpe, Fitzroy Simpson,
and Lloyd Ferguson. Their specialty is militant lyrics set to achingly sweet music, sung
with a naïve harmonic mastery that has made
them the most popular trio on the island since
Burning Spear. And where Spear and the
Wailers are past masters of political reggae,
their music is often too sobersided for the
mass of Jamaicans, who care as much about
sex and nonsense as the next nationality. Into
the reggae heartthrob gap leap the Mighty Diamonds.

It's the usual story of too many failed singles for too many sleazy producers. In 1974
they had a hit with "Shame and Pride" and a
chant called "Jah Jah Bless the Dreadlocks."
They even got off the reggae track by recording a couple of soul-derived ballads originally
done by the Stylistics. But when "Right Time"
was released in early 1975 it was clear that
the young Diamonds meant business:

Marcus Garvey prophesy say
Man a go find himself against de wall
It a go bitter
When the right time come
Some a go charge fe treason
When the right time come

Some a go charge fe arson
When the right time come
Some a go charge fe murder
When the right time come

"Right Time" was a clear illustration of reggae's power over young Jamaicans. Among the Rastas and rebellious youth the song validated an attitude that when real tests come for Jamaica, as the song said, "Natty Dread will never run away." The Diamonds followed this with the gently rolling "Have Mercy" and a smooth tribute to the olden days of reggae, "I Need a Roof," a shanty dweller's lament delivered in rock-steady terms.

The Diamonds are also a good example of how reggae continually recharges itself on the strength of its traditions. Many of the Diamonds' best songs utilize standard rhythmic formats, called "riddims" by the musicians. For instance, their fresh and beautiful "Why Me Black Brother Why" was originally "Rocking Time," by Burning Spear; "Have Mercy" was "Why Did You Leave Me," by the Cables; and "Natural Natty" was originally a deejay record by Prince Jazzbo. Reggae telescopes in and out of itself, continuing trends from other records. "It's not like we stealing anything from anybody," Tabby says. "We take a riddim and update it and rerecord it. And then we apply our new ideas to it. We call it 'anointing' the riddim with our own magic."

In the summer of 1976 the Diamonds signed with a British record label, Virgin (as did U Roy), and toured the States with the Maytals. On their opening night in Boston, the three young dudes strode out on the stage waving machetes. They wore red and gold

The Mighty Diamonds at home

The Mighty Diamonds

zoot suits and put on a terrific show, segueing smoothly from one hit to another in spite of the occasional sabotage of Toots's backing band, which didn't want to see the Diamonds blow the Maytals off their own stage. The Diamonds performed gawky soul steps, hunched into swinging mojo crouches, and wound up with a high skip-stepping offstage routine. They were incredibly energetic and professional. With Big Youth, the Diamonds must be the reggae act to watch. Backstage they quickly stripped off their suits and changed into street clothes, sweaty and clowning with a spliff. Someone said that the machetes scared the audience. The next night they were dropped from the show.

Drive out of Kingston down Molynes Avenue on the hottest day of the winter; cut left on Washington Boulevard to get to Lee Perry's yard in Washington Gardens. It's rush hour and the buses, packed like Japanese subways, are careening down the boulevard raising clouds of red dust. Young girls with onyx eyes offer bags of bittersweet tamarind seeds for sale in the street. Thousands stream along on foot, leaving the hot whirlpool for the surrounding shantytowns, the suburbs, the country.

Lee Perry is another reggae chieftain. As a producer, he was responsible for the earliest and best Wailers recordings, earning partial or full writing/composing credits for some of Bob Marley's best songs. He started the Upsetters, one of the great Kingston studio bands. A producer like Lee Perry can keep a studio band like the Upsetters (or the Aggrovaters, or Skin Flesh and Bone) in the studio all night and within a month have twenty singles released from that one session, for which the musicians are paid about fifteen dollars per man per song. Perry also produced Marley's Selassie-affirming "Jah Live," which sounded cruder and consequently better than most of the Wailers' self-produced recent work. Perry also records deejay music (whose main lyrical concern seems to be Colombian marijuana) under the *nom de dub* Jah Lion.

He lives in the tract suburbs. Cows, horses, goats, and sheep wander the streets and graze. A sign warns that roaming pigs will be destroyed. Behind his house is a green cinderblock structure—Perry's studio, called the Black Ark. Inside, in the control booth, Perry is performing an imperious ritual on a red, green, and gold carpet before his studio console. He wears a red-striped undershirt rolled up to his chest. In the process of flamboyantly mixing a dub version of "Super Ape" by the Upsetters before a mesmerized crowd of hangers-on, Perry spins and twirls and punches knobs on a sixteen-track mixing board. The room is filled with electrostatic drone as the speeding tape spools are geared

PRESSURE DROP

F. HIBBERT

down again for another take. He punches in a voice track and steps on it with the reverb. What comes out is the sound of the light at the end of the tunnel. Something like that, anyway. Dub can get pretty weird, and Lee Perry is its most radical sorcerer.

Inside the dark studio a few musicians were watching eight-millimeter pornographic films pojected on a small screen. Perry was satisfied with the mix of "Super Ape" after the thirtieth take. He looked over and growled amiably that he was too tired to talk. From his console he flipped on the studio lights and yelled into the mike, "Moxie! Weh Mox?" Sitting inside was Max Romeo, the thirty-year-old singer who for ten years has been an eccentric force in the reggae world. His penetrating tenor bites into a song with unique ferocity, and his martial "War ina Babylon" was a huge success in Jamaica until the song was banned from air play when the Jamaican Government declared a state of national emergency in the summer of 1976. Max tells his own story:

"I don't want to give you too much of the political side because I'm afraid of that word. Politics are my greatest fear."

You did write a song about socialism. . . .

"Yes, but it was about socialism as a concept, not a political party. Not like Cuban socialism or anything else. To me socialism means to socialize. To me, socialism means love."

The government used your song for its election campaign. . . .

"But I didn't write it for them. They just took it from me. The inspiration was not political in nature. Politician use you for whatever purpose to get himself elected, y'know? I am from the ghetto. And I socialize with people who suffer a lot. Nights without place to sleep, days without meals and you can't go out because you can't afford shoes or pants and to go in certain places you must be dressed in this society to be able to see what a-guan on. And even if you have no clothes and if your pride

overcome your fear and you say, 'Forward,' well, you get kicked out. It's what you call lack of opportunity. Suffering. And so I'm always inspired by inner feelings that direct my outer action. And right now the only inspiration that come is to write about suffering people. I also suffer. Just like they."

You used to sing mostly about sex.

"And now I sing about poor people, and whenever you sing about the poor people you sound like a politician. Do you dig what I mean? People listen and say, 'Moxie singin' fe politic,' but I'm not! I'm just telling what is happening to my brothers and sisters. Dig?"

How did you get started in music?

"As what you'd call a handyman. Y'know, little guy that carries the records around and say, 'How 'bout dat?' and 'You like dat?' to the guys in the record shops and then take the

Max Romeo

orders back to the boss. That's how it was for me in those days, '65, '66, somewhere around there. I was seventeen years in age. And I used to like to sing so I took a job where it might happen for me, y'know? And so one day I'm singing and the boss say, 'Ya got good voice quality, bwoy. How 'bout tryin' a t'ing?' And I went that night and call a couple of guys and put the idea to them to help me write a song. It was called 'Buy You a Rainbow.' I used the same two guys on harmony and we called ourselves the Emotions. Song did well, y'know. Went to number two on the two radio stations at the time."

How does a musician survive in such a competitive atmosphere?

"Well, it's a rat race. Man writes a song, got twenty places where he can go rent a studio and record it, got a pressing plant next door and easy to distribute. There's not a lot of legal holds on what you can do and people naturally steal from the musicians. Some guy will be smart and won't make a record without getting a fifteen-cent royalty—you write it down on a piece of paper and you get your royalty check. And some other guy will be so hungry to go into the studio he forgets to make an agreement and the producer take advantage of him. And that's the way it is. Depends on the musician."

You're famous for a song called "Wet Dream" that was very big in England in 1969. It was number two until it was banned by the BBC for its suggestive lyrics. . . .

"Yeah. That's an image I'm trying to shake off. It was a hit and I got a tour out of it in 1970 all over England. Cities, towns, as far as Cardiff. But I was embarrassed because the lyric was about making love, and I had to tell the respectable people that it was about a leaky roof. My problem is people are still looking for the same kind of thing from me and I'm trying to make a new course.

"Down here in Jamaica we traveling on the road we like. It's called liberty. Jamaicans like

to be free. Doesn't matter what it cost. And we like to be recognized as people by men, so that a man can go into the Sheraton without them giving the eye over the shoulder and saying, 'Oh he's from Kingston 12 [Trench Town]. Whass he doin' in Kingston 2?' Because Kingston 12 is the ghetto and Kingston 2 is the new city and it like a man has to cross a border to get there. Because a man wearing crocus bag [burlap] and ain't smelling of Avon they say, 'Whass he doin' here?' "

When we stagger into the Sheraton they say the same thing.

"People should realize that people are people regardless of what they have. What you have don't give you nine feet of earth when you die and me six foot six when I die. Six foot six is due to everybody. Except for inflation—eeheeheehee—soon we all get maybe t'ree foot six. Everyman's a man and everyman desire what is given to him, which is life. And ya live. Dig? And you live in love and unity. Break your bread when I ain't got any and I'll break mine when the time come. This is what I preach."

Are you a Rastafarian?

"Yeah, mon! Rastaman is the only man who know love in Jamaica. We get kicked around for it. We get thrown in jail for it. But soon the world will be cryin' for it. Even first time when you meet a Rastaman in the street he announce it as a greeting: 'Love, brother.' Love all around. Him hungry and can hardly dig, but still it's 'Hail Niya! Love!' All Jamaican youth copy Rasta now. It's the fashion."

Among Romeo's many hits are "Three Blind Mice," "Let the Power Fall on I," "Revelation Time," and "No Joshua No," a stern warning to Jamaican Prime Minister Michael Manley, who is known as Joshua to the Rastas:

You took them out of bondage
And they thank you for it
You sang them songs of love
And they tried to sing with it
But now in the desert
Tired, battered and bruised
They think they are forsaken
They think they have been used
I want you to know Joshua
Rasta is watching and blaming you
Since you are my friend Joshua
I want you to forward and start
   anew. . . .

Ras Michael

10

The Sons of Negus Live in Shantytown

FIVE MORE DEAD AT OLYMPIC GARDENS DANCE

—*headline in the* Daily Gleaner

The burra drums are religious survivals from Africa, and burra is probably the oldest Jamaican musical form still extant, although the three burra instruments are now known collectively as *akete* drums. The bass drum is the largest. The repeater is smaller and higher pitched with a taut goatskin membrane. The funde is tuned flat for syncopation with a slack membrane. In Kingston forty years ago the drums were generally used for dances on holidays but also had a more specialized role in the slum communities. Discharged prisoners were traditionally welcomed back to town by feverish burra dances on the night of their release. Family and friends would join in wild circles around the newly freed man as the burra drums raged on. As the Rastafarian movement became prevalent in the ghettos and shantytowns, the burra dances were grad-

ually taken over by the Locksmen. The beat that had once reintegrated prisoners into their communities became the throb of the Rasta "groundation," the prayer meeting that is the only organized worship of Rastafari. This was a natural progression, as many common criminals in the '40s and '50s adopted the Dreadlocks for easier access to the slums. One famous Dread bad-ass was named Woppy King, a rapist and gangster who was finally captured and hanged. As late as 1958 two incidents were reported in Trench Town of Rastas throwing infants into bonfires as sacrifices. Eventually the old burra dance was replaced by the Niyabinghi dance, whose doctrine was "death to white and black oppressors."

Numerous drumming brotherhoods evolved in the neighborhoods; of these several developed into Rasta performing bands. The most

141

Ras Michael and the Sons of Negus

famous is Count Ossie and the Mystic Revelation of Rastafari, a troupe that dispensed burra drumming and Rasta lore before Ossie's death in 1976 and represented Jamaica at Carifesta, the annual pan-Caribbean music and arts festival.

Ras Michael and the Sons of Negus, using the burra rhythms as their foundation, lay on electric instruments and modern reggae sensibility, building a hybrid of old and new. They have an album out in Jamaica called *Rastafari* and are extremely popular. It is said that the ground swell of reggae popularity begins with the children. If the kids are bopping around singing a tune after they hear it on the radio once or twice, a huge hit is almost guaranteed. Nearly every kid under ten we met in Jamaica knew the words to Michael's hit

"None A Jah Jah Children No Cry." As it turned out, Ras Michael and the Sons of Negus not only developed a rambling, jamming style of play until they seemed like the Grateful Dead of reggae, but they also supplied bubble-gum music for youth as well.

Late one night we were in our hotel watching American police shows on Jamaica's lone television channel. Earlier the Rasta elder Mortimer Planner, accompanied by several drummers, had appeared on the Top of the Pops and croaked out a song called "Sons of Gentry." A knock on the door revealed Kiddus-I, of the Neguses, Ras Michael's factotum. We were summoned to the rehearsal we had been invited to a few days earlier. Live reggae being rare in Jamaica, we didn't hesitate although there was some reluctance to trust Kiddus with our lives since he said we were going into the ghetto and tribal warfare had been increasing. We followed Kiddus' borrowed Volkswagen through the deserted avenues, down into the western gut of the city through back alleys and tin-sided dirt streets. We wound up in an open-air body shop and a group of shadow figures surrounded the car. After some negotiation a half pound of ganja was bought for the musicians for $8. We asked Kiddus where we were and he answered, "Welcome to Olympic Gardens." It was the worst area of gang terrorism in Jamaica; we remembered the morning paper's headline and several times thought this night could conceivably be our last.

Kiddus took off again, his tires screaming as he rounded curves on two wheels. A tortuous series of rights and lefts put us into the heart of Shantytown. It was midnight and the streets were empty. The headlights revealed a hungry moonscape of tin, cement, and spit. The atmosphere was acrid with fumes and smoke. From a few blocks away came the muffled roar of an electric band with thunderous rhythm. As we drew nearer the sound we could see yellow light blazing through the windows of a tin-roofed clap-and-shout church. Dozens milled around outside despite the late hour. Kiddus pushed his way into the building, which was packed with tiny black children on wooden benches and Ras Michael and the Sons of Negus, augmented that night by the best session musicians in Jamaica, blaring out their songs at top volume.

The name of the place was The Church Is One Foundation Church. The walls were red, green, and gold. Ras Michael, barefoot, handled the microphone and sang in a hard, clear tenor that matched the static electricity of his band. In front of him were the ragged Sons of Negus we had seen at Chela Bay, seven wasted-looking hand drummers who sat like a line of Benin bronzes, expressionless, in total communion with the heartlike Rasta beat. Up

Ras Sidney

on the altar, wedged between amps and speakers, were Earl "Chinna" Smith, the top reggae guitarist who plays with the Wailers, Burning Spear, and on everybody's records; Robbie Shakespeare, the great bassist of the Aggrovaters and the Black Disciples; drummer Carlton Lee; and Geoffrey Chung on keyboards. These were the best reggae had; they were cooking and had been for hours. Heaping paper plates of chicken and steaming rice were passed to the children by their mothers; this event had been billed in the neighborhood as an open rehearsal and church social for the children. The most dense, complex reggae band we had ever heard was improvising for a hundred babies, their mothers, and some journalists.

Chinna

church to see what was happening. At a government youth dance two streets away on the previous night three girls had been killed during a shoot-out with toughs from the goon squads of the opposition. In the middle of his trance Ras Michael saw the scowling soldiers and snapped out of it, changing the riff by the inflection of his voice. He pointed to the soldiers and chanted, "Jah is with us" until they skulked away like rats or evil spirits.

Eventually the electric musicians had

Ras Michael went through his current hits and every child sang along at top voice— " 'None-a-Jah-Jah-chil-dren-no-cry' "—until the youngest were rocked to sleep in their mothers' arms. Then "Birds in the Treetop," "In Zion" (to the tune of "On Broadway"), "Run Come Rally," and "Rastaman Chant." Every child knew and sang all the words, and soon it was two in the morning. Between songs Michael would yell, "JAH" into the microphone until the children answered in equal volume. Then Michael would assume a sermonizing stance, gazing at his flock of lambs, crooning, "Jah! Jah Rastafari Haile-I Selassie-I. It's no secret what Jah can do."

At one point in the middle of a frenzied drumming passage a patrol of soldiers and police, attracted by the music, poked into the

enough, pulled their plugs, and started to pack their instruments. But the seven Sons were still into it. They played pure hypnotic burra for another half hour before it hit that the electric players had gone home. Afterward we were invited to hang out at the back door of one of the musicians' houses and lick the chalice. A hot soup was served, thick pepper pot with hunks of fatty goat and boiled chocho. It was prepared so hot the spine straightened involuntarily after the first spoon. Ras Michael was still cranked up and wired from his performance, and in the flickering shadows of the house delivered another long teaching on the true-born Rasta path to salvation. Michael, exalted and in song, told Peter Simon he was the reincarnation of Simon Peter, the rock on whom Christ founded his church.

Michael was concerned lest we think the power of Haile Selassie had diminished with his passing. "Haile Selassie not dead," he corrected. "Him only appear and disappear. What is death to him? *Nothing.* I get a vision of him the other day when the government say him dead. His Majesty was sitting like this in a chair. I mon look to him and say, '*Dada!*' And him turn to me and say, 'They say I'm dead, but I cannot die. I am not dead. I, RASTAFARI, *LIVETH.*'"

As on cue the rest of the Sons of Negus took the spoons and spliffs out of their faces and intoned after Michael, "I, RASTAFARI, *LIVETH.*"

Michael continued, "His Majesty said, 'They tried to kill me, but I only floated through the passage of time.'"

The Sons intoned, "THEY TRIED TO KILL ME, BUT I ONLY FLOATED THROUGH THE PASSAGE OF TIME."

"It was a vision y'know," Michael continued. "Like reggae is a vision. Reggae is the

Robbie

word that hits at the heartstrings the mind can't control. I and I get the message of Rastafari out through reggae. It is the black music

line of message to the world. It is the black Rastaman line of message to the world. It is the metaphorical Black Star Line. American blacks are running from the images that reggae puts out. But they will see that one day soon Jah will put a one-hour judgment on Babylon, and that judgment will be a Dread judgment. Rasta's time is come."

Just then the chalice came around, a huge goat's-horn water pipe into which are plugged the pipe bowl and a two-foot rubber tube. Ganja and blond tobacco are chopped up and mixed in the manner of North African kif. The ideal way to smoke the chalice is to "kick it," stoking an enormous cloud of blue smoke and then inhaling the last vulcanizing lungful, holding it until the back of the skull is melted into the ganja zone. One of the Sons showed me the proper kicking technique and churned up a fulminous cloud. When it dissipated he wasn't there. They said his name was Icy B, and he vanished!

We thanked Ras Michael and made our way back to the car to find Kiddus siphoning off half a tank of gas. But we thanked him too and gave Chinna Smith a ride to his house even further out in the suburbs. We got home at dawn. The old guardian was sound asleep and we tiptoed quietly so as not to wake him.

Ras Sidney and Kiddus-I

11
I and Eye

When we formulated our plans for this book, I imagined I would photograph reggae musicians, recording studios, amps and guitars, producers, record stores and scenes at a sound system gathering. It was only after I entered that magic island that I realized how multilayered the photographic dimensions were. We plopped down on the island, fresh off a super-jet, and suddenly we were in another time and space. Everywhere I gaped there was a perfectly framed photograph staring me in the eye. I quickly realized that reggae may be the main subject of the project, but that decades of Jamaican life and culture had fused to form the ingredients that created reggae, and to limit my vision to fundamental reggae would be missing the point. This realization opened up new vistas for me, and I began shooting photographs like a crazed individual. Occasionally, I overshot my bounds, offending people who were caught in the act of being themselves. It was hard convincing some Jamaicans that I was honestly trying to capture the inherent beauty and poise that has somehow graced practically every aspect of Jamaican life. But Jamaicans are naturally suspicious of the big Nikon toted by the tourist or photojournalist—it's the same invasion. So I learned protocol the hard way; a few shouts of "bloodclot," some demands of money in return, even a few threats of possible violent repercussions. But as I calmed down, so did the Jamaicans. I had to establish a sense of trust first, the photos would evolve later.

In America, you walk down a busy street, notice people buying food at the supermarket, glance at lines waiting for the bus, others hanging out on a front porch, and you don't really make much of it. But in Jamaica, each scenario seems carefully crafted and balanced as though it were a Rousseau painting, a perfect tableau, down to the smallest detail. What accounts for this phenomenon, I cannot say for sure but I certainly had never encountered it before.

—Peter Simon

Gully Bank, Kingston

Montego Bay

Kingston

Vacancy at the Playboy Club

Kingston

Sidewalk dominoes

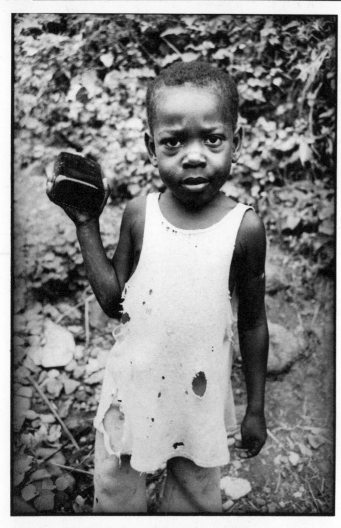

Woman with stroke foot

His belly full, but them hungry

On the way to Sunday school in Blue Hole

Hawking *The Star* in downtown Kingston

Grade school children in Maroon country

Kingston

Michael Manley

Joshua and the Rod of Correction

It takes a revolution to make a solution

—Bob Marley

The real Jamaica is usually hidden carefully from the half million or so tourists who fly in every year to enjoy the vacation spots on the North Coast. The real Jamaica is an angry, insecure Third World nation, under curfew and at war, locked in a convulsive revolutionary struggle with itself and its past. Jamaica is changing so quickly from an agro-oriented culture to an urbanized society that no one seems to be able to control the inevitable trauma. The government estimates that by the turn of the century 75 per cent of the population will be living in the island's handful of cities; Jamaica is still groping for the social and political models that will have to see the country into an uncertain future.

Politically this new Jamaica is the most important development in the Caribbean since the Cuban Revolution. The government in power since 1972 is ardently socialist and militantly reformist, and Prime Minister Michael Manley is a committed Third World visionary who would like Jamaica to be on equal terms with both capitalist and commu-nist nations. In the Caribbean today Jamaica has few parallels. Whereas Cuba is communist, Guyana has a mildly Marxist government, and the venerable socialist opposition in Trinidad and Tobago has a long history of suicide that benefits only Eric Williams, the Prime Minister, the rest of the islands are for the most part still living under the ragged thatch of tropic colonialism. With the exception of Cuba, only Jamaica has begun to seriously alter its course for the rest of the century.

But the road has been difficult for Jamaica recently. Kingston has been terrorized by brutal political violence since January 1976, when burning and looting in Trench Town were timed to embarrass the Manley government as it hosted the annual convention of the International Monetary Fund. Since then random murder and arson have escalated in frequency until Kingston has begun to take on the air of a Caribbean Belfast. Jamaica's two political parties (Manley's People's National Party and the opposition Jamaica Labor

Gun Court, Kingston

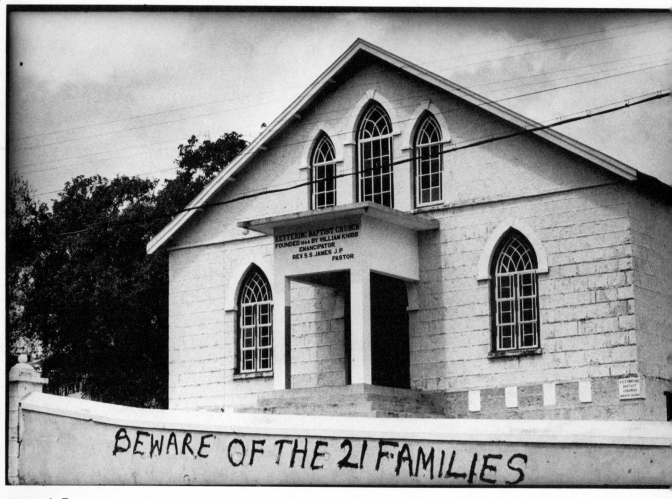

Duncan's Bay

Party) have a long history of settling arguments out of court, at night, in the grim alleys of West Kingston. Each party maintains private goon squads and gunmen, most of them in their late teens, mounted on Honda CB 200 motorbikes and armed with ratchet knives, pistols, and sawed-off shotguns.

No one knows exactly how Jamaica came to be flooded by so many guns. One theory is that the ganja traders in St. Ann and the western parishes were being paid off in millions of counterfeit dollars by American dealers who regularly fly light planes into strips hacked out of the bush to pick up their dope. The ganja traders then demanded to be paid in handguns, which could easily be sold in Kingston for cash. Another source suggests that the po-

litical parties covertly imported the weapons to arm their goon squads. By late 1974 Jamaica was being literally shot to pieces. When gunmen finally looted and terrorized the Stony Hill Hotel outside of Kingston, the Jamaica Tourist Board began to formulate a public relations scenario for when the first tourist was murdered.

That hasn't happened yet. The Manley government passed a series of emergency crime measures establishing the Gun Court, which has jurisdiction over all cases of illegal firearms. All trials are held without a jury and press coverage is barred to protect witnesses from intimidation by other gunmen. Until January 1976 a conviction drew an indefinite sentence in the sinister Gun Court prison, a stark barbed-wire structure painted bright red for maximum effect and situated in the middle of Kingston. A local court of appeal ruled the Gun Court law unconstitutional, and the government appealed to the Privy Council in London (Jamaica is still in the British Commonwealth and regards the Council as the highest court of appeal). The Privy Council upheld the legality of the Gun Court but ruled illegal the imposing of indefinite sentences. Now conviction of possessing an illegal weapon or even a few bullets draws a mandatory life sentence. And since June 1976, Michael Manley has been running Jamaica under a state of national emergency.

Perhaps the best way to gauge the Jamaican national mood is to pay attention to the rumors. During 250 years of slavery only rumor and humor kept the people going from day to day, and modern Jamaicans have developed the surviving folk art of national hearsay into high drama. While in Jamaica we were told in all seriousness by otherwise rational people that:

—A leftist guerrilla army, recruited by the People's National Party and financed by Cuba, is being trained in the Blue Mountains for a communist coup by Michael Manley;

—A rightist guerrilla army, recruited by the Jamaica Labor Party and financed by the CIA, is being trained in the Blue Mountains for a fascist coup by opposition leader Edward Seaga.

—A tightly organized force of Rastafarian brethren is camped in the Hellshire Hills outside of town with more guns that the Kingston police.

—The Cuban Friendship School, donated to Jamaica by Fidel Castro during one of Michael Manley's visits to Cuba, is being built by 135 Cuban technicians whose real purpose is to train Marxist cadres.

—Jamaica's most prominent business families, including all the Jews and most of the Chinese, are liquidating their holdings and fleeing the socialist regime for Florida and Canada.

Of these rumors, only the last has any basis in reality. Chinese and Jewish busi-

nessmen have traditionally dominated the Jamaican economy, and the government's economic reforms have cut deeply into the businessman's ability to make large profits. The result is a migration of the middle class and anybody—black or white—with the resources to leave the country. According to one businessman: "The rich and the middle class have been protected in Jamaica for literally hundreds of years. In reality they have always had their way and had never even know any real competition before. They always have been able to buy or influence their way around inconveniences, customs regulation, tax laws. But now Manley is closing up their loopholes. Because of the currency restrictions they can go to jail if they're caught with American currency. All my friends are in panic. Everybody wants to run."

The Chinese are particularly fearful. Many are the grandchildren of laborers who bought their way out of bonded servitude and opened small stores and enterprises that evolved into large concerns. During our stay one of Michael Manley's wilder political allies, Minister of Housing Anthony Spaulding, made thinly disguised anti-Asian statements saying that the Chinese were secretly sending all their money out of the country and were bleeding Jamaica dry. Since the style of Jamaican socialism is based closely on the African model, the Jamaican Chinese remember the forced confiscations and expulsion of the Asian community in Uganda very clearly. One rumor widely circulated during my stay—that the leading Chinese industrial family, the Chin Loys, were leaving the country—turned out to be true.

A current joke: Manley calls a leading Chinese executive, Mr. Yap, asking him to investigate why so many Chinese are leaving. Mr. Yap tells the P.M. that he'll meet with community leaders that night and to call him back the following day. When Manley phones the next day the maid answers and says Mr. Yap is unavailable since he moved his entire family to Coral Gables that morning.

Social turmoil is a new experience for an island that prides itself as the most politically sophisticated nation in the Caribbean. In fact, when Michael Manley and the PNP were voted into power in 1972 after the conservative JLP had sleepily governed Jamaica for a decade after independence, proud Jamaicans with an eye for statistics pointed out that theirs was the only country independent since World War II to have an orderly change of government by free election and have it stick. In 1972, Manley and his crew of social democrats inherited a notoriously corrupt civil service and a struggling young country, 90 per cent black, a West African colony, for all it seemed, that suffered a national inferiority complex right out of three hundred years of British colonialism. One veteran Kingston journalist observes: "When Manley came to power, Jamaica was given one of those rare last chances a country sometimes gets. At the time we were little more than another banana republic with a squalid right-wing oligarchy

ruling us. Now one hears so much about communism and selling out to Cuba, but if the socialist programs are allowed to mature we'll have the chance to become an austere but free and outspoken society of the left. All one can say about those who run to the States is that they're cowards and we're not that sorry to see them go."

Michael Manley was born in Jamaica in 1925. He served with the Canadian Air Force during World War II and later studied under the great socialist teacher Harold Laski at the London School of Economics. Upon his return to Jamaica, Manley was groomed to assume the leadership role of his father, Norman Manley, who founded the PNP in 1938 and proclaimed it a socialist party two years later. The younger Manley became an effective organizer of the PNP-affiliated labor union and later entered politics determined to appeal to diverse elements of the electorate, especially the young and the poor. In his rise to power Manley displayed a dazzling facility with both the intellectual (writing on emerging nations in *Foriegn Affairs*) and the mystic. In the mid-Sixties he traveled to Ethiopia to confer with Haile Selassie, living God to the estimated seventy thousand Rastafarians.

Manley's Ethiopia visit was a calculated move. He invited Selassie to visit Jamaica, and during his stay the Emperor presented Manley with one of his white imperial staffs as a gift. In the eyes of the Rastas and the young and country folk who were attracted to them, this gave Manley a moral authority deriving from the divine Emperor himself. The white staff came to be called the Rod of Correction, and Manley was then known as Joshua, who would lead his people after his father, like Moses, had delivered Jamaica from its colonial bondage.

Manley used his association with Selassie and the Rastas to his advantage. Jamaica is a fundamentalist, Bible-oriented society, and when Manley campaigned in the countryside

Bauxite works, near Alexandria

brandishing the Rod of Correction, country folk would fall on their knees, shouting, *"Joshua! Joshua Stick!"* Jamaica's most popular reggae musicians wrote infective hits for Manley's campaign, and the PNP eventually swept into office on Delroy Wilson's "Bettah Mus' Come."

Once in power, Manley began to alter the economic and social structure of Jamaica. Important ministries were given to young allies, mostly foreign educated with a socialist slant toward the Third World. Land reforms established co-operative farms, the largest near Montego Bay named after Tanzanian president Julius Nyerere. But the major economic factor of Manley's identification with the Third World was that Jamaica, like the Arabs had done with oil, be paid a guaranteed price for raw materials sold to industrial nations. Jamaica's price for its major export, bauxite, had always been left to the chancy fluctuation

of the free market system. But in the spring of 1974, after the rise in oil prices increased Jamaica's energy bill by $200 million and left the economy in shambles, the Manley government drastically increased the bauxite levy, the royalties and taxes Jamaica receives from the five American and Canadian companies mining its bauxite. The 300-per-cent increase staved off national bankruptcy and seemed to further the psychic alignment with the Third World.

But Manley struck out even further on his own course. To general middle- and upper-class alarm, he began a friendship with Fidel Castro, arranging cultural and industrial exchange programs. The relentless Jamaican grapevine even had Castro making secret helicopter visits to Manley's home for weekend skull sessions. Castro donated a school and sent Cuban technicians to build it. The JLP remonstrated in Parliament, asking why

Cubans had to erect the school when Jamaica was suffering from 25-per-cent unemployment. Indeed, the fear that Manley is selling himself to Cuba is rampant in Jamaica, and PNP officials are constantly touring the island reassuring business and community leaders that Jamaica is not "going communist." And in what many saw as a calculated display of his independence, Manley refused to allow Angola-bound Cuban troops to use the Kingston airport as a staging area, although Jamaica was among the first to recognize the leftist M.P.L.A. as the legitimate government of decolonized Angola.

There really is a gradual socialist revolution under way in Jamaica. As one of his supporters put it, "Manley and his crew are adventurers, Columbuses in a way. When they embarked on democratic socialism in this colonial society they had no idea what forces they would release. Now life is thrilling here where it used to be stultifying and dull. You can feel in the air that history is being made."

I had the opportunity to speak with Michael Manley during a particularly tense period for his government. Longshoremen of the JLP-affiliated union had walked off the piers in carefully orchestrated wildcat strikes, and the island faced severe shortages of rice, cooking oil, and soap. The previous night Manley had gone to the docks and used all the resourcefulness of his years as a labor leader to persuade the strikers to unload the ships. The crisis had abated somewhat.

We met in his office at Parliament. A man given to dramatic gestures, Manley is tall, close-cropped, and athletically built. When he stood up to shake hands he seemed to radiate a regal authority and confidence. His brow often furrows as he is thinking and when he smiled he had the face of a good-natured Creole Jove. He speaks without pausing, and his ideas flowed with a remarkable precision and clarity of thought. He was wearing a blue

kareba suit, the open-necked, loose-fitting African garb he popularized in Jamaica in line with Third World fashion. He asked what I had been doing and wanted to know to whom I had spoken. He then eagerly launched into a spirited defense of his government, as if he had been called upon to do it often.

"We are a socialist government, not a communist one as has been so often written," he said. "We have truly incredible red-baiting here in Parliament and the press. We are primarily interested in social progress and public welfare. No matter how difficult our economic condition is today, it would be far worse if we hadn't instituted the social progress we put through two years ago. If you walk through Trench Town this afternoon and see how our people live, I *guarantee* it will break your heart The average Jamaican worker earns twenty-five dollars a week. We have to try to create a conscious society independent of the United States, of Britain, of the Soviet Union, of Cuba, of anybody.

"Whatever problems we have with the U.S. stems from your fear of socialism. Washington doesn't even have to sneeze, it only has to feel a little chill to get scared. But we have economic pneumonia here. We must have access to *all* the political systems. As a Third World nation we have to be friends with everybody to survive. As for Cuba, we find them to be the most enthusiatic, the most hard-working, and above all the most honest to work with. We help them with tourism plans and they help us with schools and fishing technology. Right now we are working on a transshipment port for Cuba so that, say, the ZIM line can unload freight in Jamaica destined for Cuba. We think we can prove we can deal on equal terms with Cuba and Israel and anyone else. We have strong new relationships with Costa Rica and Mexico. Soon we will ship our bauxite to Mexico, where it can be smelted into alumina [the intermediate stage between bauxite and aluminum] using Mexico's inexpensive natural gas energy. We will *still* give the States the main strategic interest in bauxite. *Nothing* is aimed politically at the U.S. But we must pioneer this policy so that the price for our bauxite will be based on the price of an alumina ingot. And this excites us *terribly*. We have made our choice for the future and we are taking the co-operative route."

I asked the Prime Minister if he could effect his reforms with an aggressive opposition working to undermine him. His face clouded and he frowned.

"Well . . . we're doing it, I think. Our programs are only beginning to work now. We regret the excessiveness of the opposition propaganda. They misrepresent us to scare the middle class. But we are committed to proving you can have vigorous change and maintain the two-party system. We remain committed to democracy here. And you'll notice the JLP never suggests they would dismantle what we have done if they came to power. We admit there are bugs and imperfections, but just now you are beginning to see the *outline* of a socialist society. The opposition says we are communist, but we wish to preserve an activist private sector. Our aim is to reform business, to use the process of worker participation to resolve the adversary relationship between worker and management. You can't re-create in your economy the conditions of a world championship prizefight. We don't want another business structure like Madison Square Garden. For anyone who wants to become a millionaire in Jamaica, and I've said this before, we have five flights to Miami every day.

"We feel we must use social engineering to eliminate the errors of private enterprise here. We don't think that multinational corporations are a sound basis for agriculture and social reform. Our society should be geared to this crucial reformation between management and worker. We need for the worker to let the creative side of his persona have expression in the plant, not just on the weekend. Not to understand this is to admit the failure of what the human condition is all about."

With the Rod of Correction in mind, I asked Manley if he felt he represented a moral as well as a political authority.

"I try to keep alive my own perception of moral issues," he said with a faint smile. "In Jamaica the moral focus is too often lost to pragmatism. We have to keep a moral focus on the terrible suffering and poverty we have here. I listen carefully to the new reggae songs because they remind me that the slums are still there and that they are among the worst in the world. The middle class tells me we are moving toward socialism too fast. The reggae and the Rastas tell me we are moving too slow. My favorite song? 'I Mon Born Yi' by Pluto."

An aide stuck his head in the door and reminded the Prime Minister that he was late for another appointment. I asked if he still maintained contacts with the Rastafarian culture. "Look around you," he said, "and see what colonialism has done to a displaced people. Man has a deep need for a religious conviction, and Rasta resolves the contradictions of a white man's god in a colonial society. Sometimes I think that the only Jamaican who truly knows who he is has to be the Rastaman. They're very beautiful and remarkable people." The aide came in again. We shook hands and Manley started to run out of his office, followed by the aide, who grabbed his briefcase from him. Over his shoulder Michael Manley offered me a ride uptown. I had my own car and had to decline, but I was impressed by the typically Jamaican generosity of the offer.

I had been invited to lunch in the members' dining room at Parliament that afternoon by Neville Gallimore, a young physician and member of the opposition whose constituency is in rural St. Ann Parish to the north. As we chatted over oxtails, rice, and gunga peas, the dining room began to fill with Jamaican politicians. The previous night several policemen had been shot and the city's tensions were reflected in the coolness of the PNP and JLP politicians to each other. Political differences were also evident in sartorial style; the PNP socialists were dressed in tan and light blue kareba suits while the JLP members wore English business suits and co-ordinated Miami-chic outfits.

"Let me tell you about Michael," Dr. Gallimore said, referring, as everyone does, to the P.M. by his first name. "After his election he was so charismatic and charming. We watched him explaining his programs and ideas on television and even I and many of my colleagues said, 'May this man rule this country for many years.' He was enormously popular until he began his courtship of Cuba two years ago. Things went badly with our economy and peo-

ple began to ask questions. What had happened to Michael's management abilities? How could the economy be in such chaos that austerity measures have to be taken? Our economy grew 8 per cent in 1971. Last year the growth rate was zero. If there was control of the economy, if there was unity among the people which has been disrupted because of the introduction of foreign ideology, then we would be holding our own. If you ask what Michael has done to cause this I couldn't tell you. But all the confidence is gone. A man feels if he makes more money here he's in trouble."

We were joined by a JLP senator named Pernell Charles. Young, black, with a degree in political science from CCNY, Charles seemed like the archetypal Third World graduate student to be found on American campuses in the Sixties—angry, articulate, usually socialist in temperament. I remarked on this and mentioned that I thought it ironic to find him back home working against socialism. He answered that he generally supported Manley "until some of our political sovereignty was sold to Cuba. I couldn't go with the radical trend." While he was talking I was making notes, but he stopped me abruptly and asked me to put my notebook away. He pointed out that Security Minister Keble Munn ("our CIA") was sitting behind me. Charles looked very nervous. "You see, Manley and his gang are serious about their revolution. And anyone who has studied political science can tell you that no so-called Third World country has achieved a social revolution with an opposition. Look at Egypt under Nasser, Indonesia under Sukarno, Algeria under Ben Bella, Ghana under Nkrumah, Cuba under Castro— before they had their reform they got rid of the opposition. And I'm telling you that if Manley stays in power the same thing will happen to us."

Three months later, after the State of Emergency was declared, Pernell Charles was arrested and charged with sedition. As of early 1977, he was still in detention.

What is in store for Jamaica? The most common scenario has Manley and the PNP holding the government, but perhaps with a greatly reduced majority. One observer states, "The PNP programs in youth development, housing, and agro-industry should provide them with a more solid base, *if* they can hold out through continued violence and unrest. The alternative is deteriorating conditions and a 'nonvote' that could put the JLP back in office."

I spent one afternoon with John Hearne, the Jamaican novelist and television commentator, who generally supports the government. "I give Michael credit only for visionary leadership," Hearne said. "He knew that socialist programs had to be implemented for our national survival. No Jamaican politician ever took any risk before Michael. He was forced to go for the liberation of our psyche, for the encouragement of question. He went for broke and gave palpable self-assurance to the entire generation of young Jamaicans. Now there's no turning back for him."

My afternoon with Hearne wore on talking politics. The heat abated some and we strolled outside to smell the crisp ozone of the tropic air and watch the lights come twinkling into play from the homes of the affluent in the mountains over Kingston. Hearne looked up and a trace of bile crept into his voice as he nodded toward the winking lights high above.

"Look at those bastards up there," he said. "They live like kings and Trench Town is less than two miles away. It's a wonder they haven't all had their throats cut by now. You could call it the final tribute to the inherent patience and gentleness of the Jamaican people." The wind changed and the smoke from a bonfire drifted into the courtyard, burning our throats. Kingston is a city of fires, a city on fire, and whether the flames will be contained is the question Jamaicans are asking themselves.

Kingston

⑬

A Visit to Kali Mountain

And he showed me a pure river of water of life, clear as crystal, proceeding out of the throne of God and of the Lamb. And in the midst of the street of it, and on the other side of the river, was there the tree of life, which bore twelve manner of fruits, and yielded her fruits every month: and the leaves of the tree were for the healing of the nations.

Revelation 22: 1,2

Jamaica is widely estimated to have the highest density of cannabis users of any country in the Western Hemisphere and probably the world. Government figures and various private studies indicate that between 60 and 70 per cent of the population smokes, drinks, or ingests ganja in one form or another. Ganja use is ritualized by the Rastafarians and is essential to the Rasta cosmology. Use of the plant for psychoactive and medicinal purposes is increasingly widespread among the young Jamaican middle class, but for the most part ganja is still considered the poor man's high.

Most Jamaican smokers believe that ganja was being smoked by the aboriginal Arawak tribes when Columbus arrived in 1494. Others say that it was introduced by African slaves. The Rastafarians proclaim its divine origins. But common hemp, introduced and promoted by the British as a plantation crop throughout the New World, was unknown in pre-Columbian Jamaica. The great likelihood is that the use of cannabis was introduced to the island by the large numbers of indentured laborers from India who began to arrive in Jamaica in 1845 to work the great sugar plantations that were almost idle since Jamaican abolition in 1838. Ganja is the Hindi word for marijuana; the term is so institutionalized in Jamaica it is used in legislation and the courts. The Hindi word Kali, denoting the Black Goddess of Strength, also signifies the most potent grade of ganja. It is assumed that the indentured Indians smoked with black cane cutters on the plantations and from there the use of the plant was absorbed into Jamaican working-class life.

The use of ganja has been illegal in Jamaica since 1913, when the white planter class, vastly outnumbered by the descendants of their former slaves, voted to outlaw the smoking of ganja, the practice of *obeah,* and informal close-order drilling by blacks. For sixty years the ganja penalties have been harsh and mandatory: one year in prison for possession, two years for cultivation, five years for selling. The sentences are no longer mandatory but, to compensate, the courts often deal out the maximum term to those stupid, careless, or ignominious enough to be arrested by the mostly nonchalant Jamaican police. For years the ganja trade has been unofficially tolerated and encouraged by the police and government, who in turn benefit economically from what in several parishes is the most lucrative cash crop and nationally is an underground agro-industrial complex that lures unprecedented millions of dollars in hard foreign currency into Jamaica yearly. Every Jamaican town and village has its "herbsmen" or "bushmen," small farmers who cultivate two hundred to four hundred roots (yielding about two pounds per plant) along with other crops. Every parish has its big-time ganja trader, a sort of clearinghouse and distributor who buys up local harvests and resells to the North American dealers who fly small planes regularly into airstrips hacked out of bush and mountainsides, or put into North Coast coves in cabin cruisers. The police are tolerant as long as they get their cut in cash or ganja and no funny stories get back to parish headquarters.

Jamaican men smoke ganja in five-inch cone-shaped spliffs rolled with cornhusks or white paper. Women and children prefer green ganja tea for narcotic, medicinal, or prophylactic purposes. Ganja is often used as a food spice (especially in the preparation of pepper-pot soup). In deep rural areas like the Trelawny Cockpits, ganja is often used as an external tonic for wounds, infections, and allergies. Green ganja, usually from an imma-

ture plant, is moistened and attached to the painful area with a linen poultice that has been soaked in a preparation of ganja root extracts. This folk application has been in use in Jamaica for more than a hundred years and prefigures recent Czech and Yugoslav studies of the antibacterial properties of cannabis. Ganja is easily available. Every town has its "herb camp" or "ganja yard" where loose ganja, tightly packed in paper pokes, and spliffs are sold openly. Usually the proprietor has a radio or record player going, maintains a domino table, and sells Red Stripe beer or Dragon Stout.

It has long been assumed that the island's political parties derive much of their campaign income from manipulation of the ganja trade, and consequently for years Jamaica was wide open to foreign smugglers. But by 1973 the new socialist government of Michael Manley decided the ganja trade was slipping out

of control. The mysterious influx of thousands of shotguns and pistols into Kingston that had begun a few years earlier was attributed to the ganja traders who converted their weapons into cash in the city. There was also fear that Jamaica was turning into a transshipment port for heroin and cocaine on the way from South to North America. The Jamaican Government called in the U. S. Drug Enforcement Administration, which sent helicopters on ganja search-and-destroy missions, experimented with chemical defoliants, and erected hundreds of thirty-foot steel poles along the flat roads of Negril and the western parishes. Painted dull brown so as not to reflect searchlights, the poles are intended to shear off the wings of light planes that fly ganja missions into the deserted roads, illuminated only by a pair of motorbike lights. Faced with the machinations of the DEA, the ganja traders retrenched, shifted tactics, and are now said to be trying to develop a new breed of plant that will stretch the two ganja crops the planters get per year into three.

The major tactical shift of the ganja trade after the government crackdowns was to lower its profile. For outsiders a visit to the ganja fields isn't as easy as it once was. But one day in Kingston I interviewed a young lawyer named Valentine Lindo, and during the course of our conversation expressed our desire to visit and photograph a ganja plantation. Lindo immediately said he would show us a ganja _mountain,_ and invited us to visit his home in St. Ann Parish in the north-central part of the island, the ganja capital of Jamaica.

One midnight we roared out of a sleeping, pitch-black Kingston in Lindo's big Jaguar, a red mint 3.8 sedan, the kind of elegant old car you still see disappearing behind the embattled gates of the Liguanea Tennis Club. A vanishing species. We drove west along Spanish Town Road and turned north through the mountains, passing through deserted towns— Bog Walk, May Pen, Four Paths, Have Not. There was a full moon high in the sky with a bright yellow corona haloing it; the landscape was bright with lunar shadows. After two hours we veered off the paved road and traveled for another hour on gravel through jungle, farm country, and bauxite earth-stripping works. At four in the morning we arrived at the little country estate Lindo owns, surrounded by a tall chain-link fence. A pack of mean-looking Alsatians yelped at us rabidly on the other side of the fence until the lawyer cooled them out with soothing noises. He relocked the gate behind us and penned up his dogs before he let us out of the car.

Later, we sat out on his porch in the fresh night air, exhausted from the drive, sipping tea. The deep bush country was fragrant with oleander, ginger lily, and dew. "When you go into the mountains today you'll see that the ganja boys and the cool cats are more careful these days about who sees their crops," Lindo said. "My only advice is to be very open with them, don't do anything too fast, and do your business and get out. And above all don't buy any ganja around here because in these hills even the yams have ears and everybody knows everything." Lindo shifted his weight in his chair and something fell out of his pants pocket onto the tile floor with a metallic clatter. It was a small automatic pistol. Lindo looked somewhat sheepish as he picked the thing up and stuffed it into his waistband. Then he smiled. "Believe me, in Jamaica these days you can't be too careful."

When we awoke later that morning, we found a table had been set under a tree, and Lindo's cook fed us a Jamaican country breakfast: cornmeal porridge cooked with cinnamon, fried red plantain, boiled green bananas, instant Blue Mountain coffee stirred into boiling milk. The house was on a hilltop and boasted a long view of St. Ann, impossibly fecund and green, occasionally gouged deep red by a bauxite mine. Overhead big John Crow turkey buzzards circled in holding patterns, searching for breakfast. Graceful white cattle egrets (sea gulls, Jamaicans called them) were settled for the morning in the pastures. The air was percolating with moisture and tropic heat.

An hour later Jim arrived, a good-natured, diplomatic tenant of Lindo's who farmed a section of his land and was a respected local resident. Because of his political position Lindo couldn't go to the ganja areas himself, but he explained that Jim would see us through. Jim smiled, somewhat nervously, I thought.

We set off about noon, Jim at the wheel, riding paved roads so narrow they're not even on the map. We ran through little villages and shack towns—Aboukir, Inverness, Culloden (many of the early white planters were

Scottish), St. D'Acre; then west toward Watt Town and through Gibraltar and Endeavor. We eventually turned off the paved road onto a little dirt street, stopped at a tiny shanty bar, and parked behind a new green Toyota pickup with five huge burlap sacks in the back. Jim got out and exchanged a few words with the young man at the wheel, who was wearing mirror sunglasses and a red, green, and gold Rasta wool cap. Then Jim came back to the car and said, "Him jes' checkin' ya out, y'know." The ganja boy in the Toyota was staring at us hard through his rearview mirror.

Abruptly the Toyota gunned his engine and tore down the dirt street, leaving a spew of dust and grit. Jim began to follow at a discrete distance. The dirt street turned into a precipitous mountain track, beaten and pitted with wheel ruts. We lost sight of the pickup and Jim drove faster, hairpinning turns and dodging around herds of goats and waving uniformed school children. We went deeper into the mountains, up and down a tumultuous series of dirt roads. There was a screeching halt and another clipped conversation with the green Toyota. Another pickup arrived, this one red and loaded with more bulging sacks and several scowling young Dreads wearing Rasta gear. The green Toyota disappeared and we began to follow the red one. Jim explained that the mirror sunglasses was named Fox and that he controlled the traffic in this area. He had recently been arrested and couldn't risk being seen in his fields by strangers. The Dreads in the red pickup were his partners. Jim said that Fox was seventeen years old.

The final series of roads grew progressively more primitive. Suddenly, on what seemed like a badly washed-out roadbed, we drove quickly past a spacious, multilevel pastel villa with a new Lincoln Continental parked in the

Kali Mountain

Drinking ganja tea

The ganja vanished into the jungle

driveway. A totally incongruous sight in the mountain bush, and Jim explained that the house belonged to the former ganja kingpin of the area, Brother Wax, who in his prime made eighty thousand dollars in cash a month from the trade. Speaking deferentially, Jim told us that Brother Wax retired after he had buried five million American dollars in various caches throughout the hills.

We stopped abruptly at a roadside checkpoint, where we had to leave our car. Jim began to chain-smoke Craven "A" cigarettes. He mentioned that he'd been in this region the previous year with Mr. Lindo when their car was blockaded and stoned by some of the same ganja boys who were escorting us to their fields. Later, when Fox got into difficulty with the police, he was defended by Lindo. "Fox owe Lindo one favor," Jim said. "And today you dat favor." The pickup stopped when the road gave out at the foot of a steep path, and parked under a stand of banana trees. Accompanied by three ganja boys, we trudged up a goatpath, past grizzled farmers working small gardens and stands of breadfruit, coffee, cocoa, citrus, avocado, and what looked like pimento trees. Many were smoking as they worked. In spite of the blazing sun we climbed quickly, stopping only to sip cool rainwater from a concrete holding tank in the shade of a farmhouse. We worked our way up for half an hour until we came upon the first of the fields. About forty acres were under cultivation, stretching around the knobby hills as far as the eye could see. I asked Yubby, one of the boys, what the place was called, and he answered with a grin that revealed two solid rows of gold teeth, "Ya call it Kali Mountain." Two varieties of ganja grew in the lower field. The first, heavily laden with pollen and buds, was maturing Kali, the more potent grade and the more expensive. The second grade, broadly leafed and light green, was immature green ganja. Freshly harvested and uncured, the green ganja is cut mostly for tea and medicinal use.

Higher up Kali Mountain we came upon another field, this one full of bushweed, young pale green plants. Climbing farther, we discovered dozens of craggy gray granite outcroppings that jutted out of the moist earth at weird, awry angles. It was a volcanic formation but looked more like sculpted Atlantean ruins. Around the strange shapes grew big ponderosa lemon trees, called "cheddi" in Jamaica, bearing a yellow citrus fruit that tastes like a cross between a grapefruit and a lemon. One of the Dreads, a boy named Rupert, shook one of the trees until it spilled a cornucopia of cheddi fruit; we feasted on the sweet juice before continuing up the mountain.

Almost at the summit an airstrip had been cut out of the side of the mountain, big enough only for a light Cessna, and disguised with brush and tall grass. We were told it takes only three days to clear a strip like this, but they are usually discovered by the American helicopters and the life-span of the typical landing field is only about three weeks. Along the way down we asked our guards if they were Rastas. They doffed their caps to show they weren't wearing locks, but one said, "We *baldhead* Rastas. Clean-faced brethren."

We drove back the way we came, fast on bad roads. Halfway down we again saw the green pickup in front of a little bar. We stopped and went in to meet Fox, to thank him for letting us see his crop. We bought a round of Dragon Stout, and Fox and I compared drivers' licenses. Fox invited us into his truck, with Jim following behind in our car. An eight-track cassette in the cab blasted Ras Michael and the Sons of Negus at full volume. Fox was obviously doing well; his pickup alone is worth fifteen thousand dollars in Jamaica. We asked about his legal troubles, and he mumbled that there was an informer in his outfit, that he had been arrested but had made bail and been back in business in two days. We asked what he was going to do about the informer. The young boy blinked and answered without emotion:

"We a-go kill de mon."

Fox took us to his house at the foot of the mountain. He pulled into the shade and let down the tailgate of the pickup. The burlap sacks were still there. With a machete Fox opened one corner of the sack to show it was packed with Kali. He said he would offer us a special deal—three hundred-kilo sacks at three thousand dollars American per sack. We were in the midst of trying to explain we weren't there to buy when the rumble of an approaching motor intruded upon the silence. Quick glances stabbed the air, unspoken commands given, and the massive sacks were hoisted onto broad shoulders and disappeared noiselessly into the thick bush. Within seconds there was no sign of the ganja trade except for Fox contemptuously picking and sucking his

teeth and grooving to Ras Michael. The car, a civilian, passed uneventfully.

Over a cup of ganja tea in his house, Fox explained his policy of foreign trade: "The Englishmon is coward and him cheap too. I and I kyaan deal wit' dem. Dem got balls like little grapes. Canadian, him not cheap but him a coward also. But we love de American. American gonna tek a chance and got unlimited cash. We *love* de American. But him sometimes too dumb. Dem a-load too many crocus bags inna Cessna and mosh up when dem kyaan clear de mountain. Blood clot!" Fox laughed ruefully and sipped his tea.

Ganja tea is prepared everywhere on the island and is the major folk remedy. Rural doctors often prescribe tea for rheumatism, sleeping difficulties, and especially male impotence. Young men say they take ganja tea for prowess in bed and on the cricket pitch. As Fox's mother made it for us on Kali Mountain, the leaves and stems of green ganja were boiled in a little spring water and thickened with sweetened condensed milk. As I drank I talked with Fox's grandmother, who was cradling Fox's tiny daughter on her lap. The baby was cranky and the old lady asked for my cup. She fed a mouthful of the syrupy liquid to the child, who immediately stopped bawling and was fast asleep within a minute. The old lady grinned toothlessly and handed back my cup. I drank half my tea and was in a trance for the next twenty-four hours.

It was late afternoon and the sky was falling fast. A gray curtain of evening rain was visible in the distance, coming on relentlessly toward us. We departed to the usual Rasta salutations: "Love!" "Peace, brother!" "Guidance!"

Back on the paved road, Jim pulled over at another shanty bar. I ordered a Red Stripe and he had two double gins that he put back like a man who badly needed a drink. After a moment he wiped his mouth and spoke.

"This mus' be our lucky day."

"Why's that?"

"Because we come out of Kali Mountain alive with all our money. Believe me, dis *mus'* be our lucky day."

Much later, shortly before we left Jamaica, we met again briefly with Prime Minister Manley in the garden of his official residence, Jamaica House. His press secretary had told us that Manley would meet later in the day with a delegation of Rastafarian elders, and we asked the Prime Minister what he would discuss with them.

"It's part of a continuing dialogue," he said. "They always beg me to legalize ganja, and I have to tell them that although the majority of Jamaicans aren't against smoking ganja, the police and the middle class are too strongly opposed to think about legalization or decriminalization this year. The Rastas always give me a hard time, but I must tell them to be patient.

"I don't know. Someday somebody will jump into the breach and say, 'It's legal now.' Maybe it will have to be me." For a moment Michael Manley looked worried.

190

Brother Mann with the treaty

14
Maroon Country

"Kyaan ketch Quaco, ya ketch him shirt."
—*old Jamaican proverb, meaning take what you can get*

There is tantalizing white emptiness on the map of Jamaica, many square inches devoid of identifying red stripes and black dots. One patch encompasses most of Trelawny and St. James Parishes in the west-central half of the island; the other occupies a good part of Portland, near the eastern, or windward, coast. The white spaces signify Maroon country, a wilderness of rain forest, mountains, and huge pitted geological bowls called the Cockpits. The land is inhabited by the descendants of runaway slaves who fought a terrible guerrilla war against the British for eighty years, fighting the Crown to an exhausted draw in the end. The story of the Maroon nations is the tale of one of the fiercest, and ultimately saddest, struggles against slavery in the New World. But the Maroon spirit is a prideful inspiration to modern Jamaicans, still fighting the epic battles of underdeveloped nations against the neocolonial mentality.

The first Africans were brought to Jamaica from Angola by the Spanish in 1517. Several hundred were shipped in from West African ports throughout the rest of the sixteenth century, but Jamaica had no gold and the Spanish gradually lost interest, preferring to concentrate their colonial efforts on Cuba and Hispaniola to the north and east.

An English fleet invaded Jamaica in 1655; the conquest of the island by British troops, pirates, and privateers took five years, with the last armed Spanish resistance ceasing in 1660. During this time African slaves abandoned by the Spanish took to the hills in the Cockpits and the eastern mountain regions and formed tribal groupings for self-defense. These became known as Maroons as early as 1662. No one knows for certain the derivation of the word, but the common assumption is that it came from the Spanish *cimarrán*, meaning untamed or wild. *Marron* is the French word for runaway slave. In Spanish *marrano* refers to a wild boar.

In 1668 the new British planters replaced the local sugar cane with a superior cane from Barbados, and the entire economy of Jamaica was gradually geared to sugar production. Among the dozens of West African tribes imported by the British to toil in the cane fields, the strongest and most truculent were the Coromantee (including the Akan, Ashanti, and Fanti peoples) from the Gold Coast, the area today incorporated into Ghana. The Coromantee were usually blamed for the small slave outbreaks that occurred in Jamaica in 1684 and 1686. In 1690 a serious slave revolt occurred near Chapleton in Clarendon Parish. Responding to brutal treatment, slaves murdered the overseer and made off with cutlasses and ammunition. The revolt was put down the next day and the leaders executed, but not before dozens of slaves escaped into the Clarendon hills. Among those said to have run for freedom that day in 1690 was a young Coromantee named Cujo.

The gangs that formed in Clarendon maintained close contacts with slaves on local plantations. They formed raiding parties that swept unguarded livestock and plunder from the plantations, along with as many slaves as would join them. The Maroons became a haven for the increasing number of runaways, and preyed upon white plantations and settlements from 1690 to 1720. Maroon guerrilla leaders began to appear in this period, men with endurance and courage, the instinct to survive, and a brutal and desperate skill with weapons. One of these was Cujo, who they called the Mountain Lion.

Heavily outnumbered by their own slaves and under the constant threat of Maroon attack, the planters fortified their great houses and built them on hilltops and promontories overlooking the fields and huts of their slaves. It was the beginning of an institutional para-

noia that in some respects lingers in Jamaica to this day.

The colonial authorities responded by raising armed bands of slaves and Indians from Cuba to exterminate the Maroons. News of this reached the scattered gangs through their plantation networks, and the disorganized bands gathered into a single tribe and chose one man as a leader that embodied all the Maroon warrior virtues. After a parlay the tribes picked Cujo. On taking command he named as his captains his two brothers, Johnny and Accompong.

Cujo systematized the hit-and-run style of Maroon welfare, using the rugged, trackless hills to exhaust their attackers before destroying them. To conserve their puny stores of captured muskets and shot, the Maroons developed virtuoso marksmen known for an uncanny ability to kill from a long distance with a single shot. Contemporary journalists described the vicious cutlass battles fought between slave brigades and Maroon gangs if both sides stood their ground after the first volley. The Maroon tactic of being hacked to death rather than retreating gave them a mythic reputation among the slaves and encouraged further rebellion and more runaways. Even when the government brought in companies of Redcoats to put down the mutinies, Maroon ambushes were so sudden and devastating that word of the rebels' cunning and physical abilities were duly reported to London. Maroon stories also circulated through the British Army about how a warrior would go into frantic rolling contortions after firing to avoid the return shot. The Redcoats had never seen anything like it before.

Gradually the Maroons built permanent settlements. Cujo's band moved into the Cockpits, while a sizable group stayed in the Blue Mountains and built Nanny Town, named after a legendary Maroon matriarch who was so fierce that she caught Redcoat bullets in her teeth and fired them back through her breasts. The Maroons were in ever-present danger of

discovery by the increasingly bold Redcoat expeditions, and they developed an extraordinary lookout system based on blowing the *abeng,* a cow horn that carried for miles through the hills with complex syllabic messages and warnings.

Despite steady losses to ambushes, the British continued to harass the Maroons. In 1734, Nanny Town was surprised by a night attack; the British had dragged cannon to the heights overlooking the town and the village was destroyed, a terrible blow to the Windward Maroons. Many journeyed to the west to attach themselves to Cujo and his brothers in the Trelawny Cockpits. Cujo continued to resist. Wanting to establish a foothold in St. Elizabeth Parish, he placed a force under his brother Accompong and sent them off to build a camp which became the most important Maroon stronghold and remains so today.

The British offensives against the Maroons never let up, and the Redcoats were the toughest soldiers in the world. They gradually learned to anticipate Maroon tactics and minimize their losses. The pressure began to tell on the tribes, which often had to forage for food while on the run. After eighty years and three generations of war, both sides began to tire. Cujo was sixty years old in 1738, and had been fighting since he was twelve. When the British finally sued for peace that year after another Redcoat force was badly cut up, Cujo was ready. The old warrior gathered his forces and met the British at Petty River Bottom, near the original Maroon settlements of Old Town and New Town. It was an extraordinary meeting. Cujo, a short, proud man worn by decades of responsibility and war, and his men wore ragged clothes stained with the red dirt of the Cockpits. The British were resplendent in their red battle regalia. But, incredibly, it was the British who had come to treaty and were prepared to accept an autonomous nation of Maroon warriors in the midst of Jamaica. The treaty, concluded on March 1, 1739, granted freedom to Cujo and the westward Maroons and gave them ownership of 2500 acres of land for farming and hunting. The Maroons were also to cut roads in their jurisdiction and maintain order. But the most important clauses of the treaty bound them to "kill, suppress or destroy" all black rebels in Jamaica and return all future runaways that came into Maroon hands to their owners. These provisions illustrate how exhausted and desperate for peace the Maroons really were. Overnight their role changed from protectors of runaways to slave hunters. For years the wild, lordly Maroons had looked down on the blacks that chose to remain on the plantations; the British took full advantage of Maroon superiority and turned them into predators. Cujo was made chief of the Maroons for life. The treaty stipulated that British or colonial police had no authority on Maroon lands, an agreement that theoretically still holds.

But the treaty was one-sided and exploitative. It ensured peace but at a dreadful toll to Maroon pride. According to Jamaican historian Carey Robinson: "It was the triumph of a literate, sophisticated, cynical society motivated by expediency and gain, over an illiterate, vigorous but simple community skilled only in warfare and physical survival." It is likely that in his state of physical and emotional exhaustion Cujo could not fully comprehend the articles of the treaty and what they implied for the Maroons. In any case he put his mark to it. A Redcoat colonel and a captain signed for the Crown. A few months later, the British signed a similar treaty with the Windward Maroons led by Chief Quao, known as the "Invisible Hunter" for the daring of his plantation raids.

In the years after the Maroon treaties were signed, the tribes were left alone. A 1770 census lists only 750 Maroon men, women, and children in the Cockpits. They spoke African dialects with a mix of broken Spanish and English. They worshiped Accompong as God of the heavens and their obeah men were the

most powerful and sought after in Jamaica. Male Maroons looked for women on the plantations under the watchful eyes of the planters, who claimed that a child born to a Maroon father would be stronger and more valuable. Keeping the treaty, they continued to put down slave rebellions throughout the island. A Maroon warrior murdered the famous Coromantee rebel leader Tacky Blue in 1760. This, plus the overbearing attitude of Maroons toward those still in slavery, earned them the enmity of much of the black population. The Maroon strongholds were ruled by Maroon "colonels," who dressed for ceremonial occasions in flowing robes and brilliant feathers. Periodically disputes would erupt between the Maroons and the British or among the tribes themselves. A dispute over the possession of Cujo's original treaty began in 1795 between the Trelawny Maroons and the Accompongs, who had the treaty and claimed the right to keep it.

That same year, the Trelawny Maroons came into conflict with the British that ended in their exile. The white planters in Jamaica still lived in constant terror from insurrections that could begin with innocuous incidents. The 1739 treaty, splitting the Maroons and the slaves, was the greatest stroke of the colonial administration. In 1795 two Trelawnys stole a pig in Montego Bay, were caught and publicly whipped in spite of a treaty provision specifying that justice to Maroons would only be dealt by Maroons. Maroon pride was hurt and the Trelawnys, still warlike, began to send out raiding parties. They were defeated by the British in 1796, and the several hundred Trelawny Maroons were deported by ship to Halifax, Nova Scotia. Four years later, those who survived the Canadian winters were transported to the new territories of Sierra Leone, on the West Coast of Africa. Some of their descendants eventually returned to Jamaica in the nineteenth century, but of the original deported adult Maroons, none came back.

They continued to practice their traditional polygamy and to worship Accompong, and gradually were integrated into the life of their adopted country.

When the Trelawny Maroons were deported, Trelawny Town reverted to the bush and is almost lost today. But the other Maroon hamlets, Moore Town in the east and Accompong and Maroon Town in the west, are still centers of Maroon life and are relatively unvisited by outsiders. While we were staying on the North Coast we heard that a new road had recently been completed to previously inaccessible Accompong, and we decided to travel into the heart of the Maroon nation.

We left Duncan's Bay early in the morning as the fishermen were returning with their catches. We drove up and south, away from the flat seacoast and into the mountains, and rode all morning through cane fields and banana plantations, traversing broad valleys and hill ranges in making our way to Cockpit Country. Through tiny towns and settlements named Good Design, Barbeque Bottom, Ramgoat Cave, Warsop, Troy, Balaclava, Siloah, Appleton, Retirement, and the rail depot of Maggotty. Past a village called Quick Step. Another called Me-No-Send-You-No-Come. Through the parishes of Trelawny and St. Elizabeth. Through the district of Look Behind. Through that mysterious white space on the map.

By the time we reached Maggotty we were deep in the Cockpits, the steep, bowl-shaped

depressions of glens separated from each other by gigantic towers of rock carpeted with dense forests, of palm and palmlike mountain cabbage, African tulip, and poinciana trees. After pausing in Maggotty we began an hour-long ascent of the hills around Accompong, only five miles away. Winging precipitously around the alternately bright and dark ridges, we understood how the Maroons held off the British patrols that had to cut through the implausible brush. At times the air was completely still as we passed; at others the silence was split by the screams of birds and unseen animals. If you listened hard you could almost hear the far-off wail of the abeng telling the Accompongs we were on our way, although it really wasn't necessary since we had telegraphed ahead.

The road up to Accompong was beaten and pitted for most of the way as it traveled up the mountain with a thousand-foot drop, straight down, off to one side. Halfway up the road was improved, graded with crushed white rock courtesy of the U. S. Agency for International Development. As we neared Accompong we encountered young, semi-Dread Maroon warriors moving rocks around the road, making a light payday at the expense of the Americans.

We were welcomed by Brother Mann O. Rowe, an erect, wrinkled elder who is the hereditary Secretary of State of the Maroon nation. Brother Mann directed one of his sons, Jubie, to show us the village, and we followed a youth with an ebony, heavily muscled back who took us on a walking tour, swinging his machete with authority as we strolled. Ac-

Rock breaker lady on road

In Accompong

compong turned out to be like any primitive mountain village with its customary beauties, hardships, diseases, jealousies, and feuds. The major argument among the Maroons these days is over ganja. Traditionally the Accompong Maroons had used their legal autonomy to claim special privileges, including the right to cultivate ganja in exemption from Jamaican laws. But in 1957 the government denied the Maroons their ganja rights after a much-publicized lawsuit, and the Maroon ganja farmers had to move underground for the first time. What was once a united tribe is now separated by generations. The younger Maroons are attracted to the ganja trade and are supported by Brother Mann. The current Maroon chief, Colonel Wright, is against the trade and the dilution of Maroon heritage through Rasta. Several years ago Colonel Wright called in parish police to settle a dispute, the first time outside authority had been seen in Accompong in three hundred years. Once the police felt they had a mandate from the Maroon hierarchy to patrol the Cockpits, they built semipermanent stations and the epic history of Maroon autonomy was virtually fin-

ished. Now thousands of bales of ganja are rotting in the caves; the young warriors are sullen and turning increasingly to Rasta for solace and escape. The new Maroon elections were a month off when we arrived in Accompong. Brother Mann was campaigning against the conservative administration, and was heavily supported by the Maroon youth. He was planning to win and resume large-scale ganja cultivation as soon as he took office.

It was almost two o'clock when the blistering attack of the sun forced us to seek shelter in the cool of Brother Mann's ancient stone house. He cracked open the bottle of Appleton rum we had brought. His gnarled old number-one wife sulked out on the porch, peeling ginger, because she didn't get a bottle of her own.

Brother Mann took a monstrous spliff from one of his sons and inhaled a withering long draw. "This," he exhaled, "is *delicious*. I'm usin' dis fe arthritis on my leg." Another big draw and an infernal exhalation. "Good for mind too, y'know. I calls it the Wisdom Weed." After pouring himself three fingers of white rum and sweetening it with an inch of cool coconut water, Brother Mann proceeded to take out his well-thumbed herb handbook and read the entire entry under cannabis aloud.

After three more coconuts had been opened and inverted into a teapot with more rum, Brother Mann began to tell Anansi stories. The Westward Maroons are the last repositories in Jamaica of true African culture, mostly in the form of ceremonial rhythms and nursery songs. But the Anansi stories are still told among the older people, fables of heroes and animals motivated through witchcraft and sorcery. Anansi is a spider in most of the stories; he was and is the central folk culture hero of the African Gold Coast. But the Anansi story encompasses any tale of the supernatural, and this is a verbatim transcript of one story dictated word-for-word so I could write it down.

"In the old days our Captain Cujo had many brothers. They were Ashantee, Johnny, Accompong, Coffee, Quaco, Nina and Quankee. Ashantee made use of Veni-Vidi-Vici, and flew back to Africa. Quankee was a great magician and scientist but he was criminal-minded and envious. He thought that every female child was his gift from God. Quankee killed all the male children of the Maroons so he could lead the tribe through sexual intercourse. Then one day his brother Nina say, 'What dis one do if my brodder kill all de young children, dat is too terrible because we will need soldiers in the time of war.' And he decided to kill his brother to save the tribe. One gracious day he drew his sword out of its shield and cut off his brother's head. Quankee's head drop one way and the headless corpse drop the other. But the head quick jumped back on the body, intending to rejoin. It could not.

"The second time the head try to jump back on the body it cannot. Because Nina was also a scientist and he rubbed his sword with something like okra, knowing in this way Quankee could not come back to life again.

"And Quankee gave the utterance from his head: 'Ah, bwoys, ya don' tek me fair play.' And he gave up the ghost. In spite of that, there was fear that if they buried the body and the head together in one corpse, per adventure they might be joined again. Therefore the one body carried two burials. The head was buried on the cliff on that hill [he points], and the other part of the body was buried at our former residence called Old Town, one mile apart."

Brother Mann O. Rowe is fifty-eight years old and claims to have sired fifty children. He told us that his position as hereditary Secretary of State included the duty of keeper of the treaty. From a drawer in his bedroom Brother Mann produced Cujo's original copy of the Maroon treaty. The treasure was stained and wrinkled, preserved between two sheets of cheap plastic. The script and the signatures of the two British esquires were still legible, though the rubbing of the generations had long since obliterated the Maroon warlord's mark. This was the piece of paper that ended eighty years of guerrilla war in Jamaica. In spite of its many contradictions the treaty was still a symbol of exhilarating courage and the spirit of human freedom. Examining the paper in Brother Mann's parlor sent shivers down our backs. The crumpled document seemed to resonate until it was gently laid back in its drawer.

As we sat working on a brown hemp-paper spliff, a cry of warning was heard from down the road and in a flash the ganja was put away and the smoky air fanned frantically. A parish police jeep pulled up, an intrusive symbol of Jamaican authority. It was a policeman in sports clothes also named Rowe, a Maroon and a cousin of Brother Mann's. He said he was there to talk to Brother Mann's son Jackie about a stabbing. The old wife cursed him out without effect. "Ya mon was yi talkin' fe him yesterday and de day before dat." But Jackie had dematerialized into the thick bush as soon as the jeep had been sighted. The boy flew down the hillside like a demon, his jacket in one hand and machete in the other.

Accompong, it turned out, was still in the process of recovering from their annual celebration of Cujo's birthday—January 6—which had occurred more than three months previous. On that day five thousand Rastamen from all corners of Jamaica converged on Accompong to pay homage to the Maroons. For a dozen nights the Dreads took over the town, smoking, chanting, drumming, gambling.

The Rasta convention had a deep effect on the young Maroons, and many seemed to be letting their hair grow into short, modified locks. At Maroon dances one only sees the old people. At Accompong they get out an old captured red coat for special dances, riddled with bullet holes and still boasting cutlass tears.

Before we departed Brother Mann gave us his blessing and delivered a long discourse on the nature of God. "Our strength walks with you," he called to us as we drove off. Looking for a shortcut home, we turned off the AID road too early and spent two hours threading our way through the Cockpit tracks. On the back roads of Maroon country, night fell and it took five hours to get fifty miles to home.

Brother Mann O. Rowe

George, an Accompong
Maroon, with his daughters

Fred Locks

15

Labberish

Labberish is Jamaican for idle gossip; and everywhere you go in Jamaica the labberish adds up to the fact that the old days are gone forever, and good-riddance. Errol Flynn's fabulous old estate near Port Antonio is a banana plantation. Noël Coward's elegant house is maintained as a museum. No longer is Jamaica a place where the third and fourth sons of the British aristocracy are sent to make their tropical fortunes and retired civil servants like Ian Fleming can live on the cheap and write novels. Socialism has driven the wealthy and glamorous to the Bahamas. Reggae, the black Rasta message line, has taken over and the whole country jukes along to the insidious rhythms. And—this is what's really amazing—*nobody* has any idea of what's going to happen next. In the morning you hear that Jamaica is a powder keg with a lit fuse that's burning shorter every day. In the afternoon a white Jamaican who's lived on the island all his life tells you, "There could never be a revolution here. In Detroit if a man runs out of money he freezes and starves. But in Jamaica he just sits under a tree and waits for the fruit to bounce off his head. There's a pressure valve in the tropics. Who would go out and fight? The life-style of the Jamaican peasant is one of the highest standards of living in the world. And the man in Trench Town is there because he wants to do a city trip. He's usually running down a bad thing and could be back in the country if he really wanted to."

The potential power of the film-maker to influence events in a country like Jamaica is enormous. *The Harder They Come* became the reggae industry, not only reflecting it but reshaping it. Because of the movie, the music is getting through. Because the music is getting through, the messages and images of Rastafari and Third World consciousness are beaming into North America and the rest of the world.

Perry Henzell, the man who made *The Harder They Come,* is literally the Jamaican film industry, but he hasn't made a film since 1971. He finished half of his second film, *No Place like Home,* before he ran out of money. Now he's working on his third, an apocalyptic scenario that pits all the diverse elements of Jamaican society against each other in the twilight of colonialism.

The Harder They Come was made after Henzell spent most of his career making commercials. A group of Jamaican businessmen put up the money and Henzell received support from the government even though he supported the opposition party, which is now in

Coconut Cove, Negril

power. Since Henzell prefers to work without a script, using nonactors, the film was often delayed when one of the principal players got killed, or arrested, or just disappeared for a couple of weeks. Once or twice the government didn't like what was being shot and closed the production down until Henzell changed his style. The film was a critical success everywhere it was shown, but distribution was haphazard and the original backers didn't recoup their investment. Since then, with Jamaica's besieged economy, funds have been hard to find.

Perry Henzell's house is in an area of stately mansions and gardens in New Kingston. It epitomizes the brilliance of life in the tropics, wide open to the crisp ozone of the afternoon air. His office is on the bottom floor of his house. The work area is walled with wooden screen which can be opened for a tentlike at-

mosphere. In back is a small editing laboratory. Masses of lush foliage sway in the breeze and the scent of perfume is everywhere. When Henzell tires of the city he retreats to a seventeenth-century stone redoubt on four acres overlooking Runaway Bay on the North Coast.

We met for lunch in his living quarters above the office. Lunch was "poontyandup" soup, thick with white yam so the spoon stands up in the bowl, curried goat, and Red Stripe beer. Henzell spoke about his films in a soft Caribbean lilt.

"When I first started making commercials here I built a studio on a co-operative basis with Federal Recording, both for film and records. So I was always there. I remember when Millie Small used to hang around the back door. The music was completely impossible to ignore. You recognize vitality when you see it,

Perry Henzell

even if it's in a two-bit studio in Trench Town. Very early I realized that something very strange and extraordinary was going on."

Henzell is now trying to interest Michael Manley in having the government finance his new film, *The Power Game*, which sets off Jamaican politicians, the media, reggae musicians, and Rastas against each other during the struggle for control of the new Jamaica. The characters are amalgamations or caricatures of nearly every prominent figure in Jamaican life. But since Henzell doesn't like scripts it's impossible for him to say what his vision of the Jamaican power struggle will be.

"Right now I only have a story that tests certain theories I have about what is going on here now. I think you must constantly change your script to take into account changing conditions. The basic idea of communications is that for the person communicating, it's an act of discovery. It's far too simple these days just to have an idea and want to put it across. In the process of working you always discover too many things that change your assumptions."

Philip Jackson is a disc jockey with a reggae show three nights a week on Radio RJR. After ten years on the air Jackson left radio for two years, grew Dreadlocks, and went into the "Rasta cities" to follow the teachings of various Dread masters, including a powerful elder named Welder. When he re-entered society he was determined to be a sort of public relations man for Rastafari. Now his show specializes in Rasta music—Count Ossie and the Mystic Revelation, Ras Michael. "Not the hit parade stuff," he says, "but music for the Dreads out on the gullybanks. He says he decides what to play from the feedback of the record shops and sound systems. He thinks Bob Marley is making it in the outside world more because of his life-style and locks than his music. His favorite reggae masters are Big Youth and U Roy.

Don Topping is the top disc jockey in Jamaica. He played the role of Numero Uno, the deejay in *The Harder They Come* who refused to play Ivan O. Martin's record because it wasn't approved by the kingpin producer Hilton. "That's show business," he told Ivan with a shrug. "And no business, no show." Topping has been around for years and seems to have a unique perspective; he's one of the few people who have any kind of line on where Jamaican culture is going. He realizes how powerful the music is to politicians anxious to manipulate opinion and votes.

"In the last election reggae was used heavily on both sides, because the politicians are very aware of the power of the messages of these songs. They reflect the signs and feelings of the times. The person who controls music in Jamaica to a certain extent controls a huge mass of public opinion.

"The growth of reggae is incredible if you plot it on a chart. In a year, year and a half, it could be quite a force to reckon with. For the success to continue, the front-line artists, the pioneers, have to keep on producing at a high level and performing at a high level. The public must be given what it wants. One or two of them might have to modify their acts to gain wider acceptance, and those behind will have

to tighten up. There is a vast number of reggae musicians who are good players but not good performers. The Third World band has made a big impression on me, and I play Zap Pow and Ras Michael these days too. The Third World band is big with only the most sophisticated elements of Jamaicans. Big Youth? If his style goes, he goes with it, 'cause he's tried straight singing and it hasn't worked out so well. Burning Spear is like what Toots and the Maytals used to be. Lots of raw talent.

"So many Americans hear reggae music up there and they want to come down here to check it out. So they buy the records but find that Bob Marley isn't playing anywhere, Toots isn't playing anywhere. They go into a hotel lounge and they find a calypso band playing "Island in the Sun." The reggae artists still don't have a place to play that will give them a fair deal. We all say that a lot is going to have to change around here before reggae music really grows up."

Yet you occasionally find transcendence even in the hotel lounges. One night at the Coconut Cove Hotel in Negril a candle-lit outdoor meal was accompanied by a little show. First a couple of dancers came out and swirled their crimson dresses. Then a skinny Dread india-rubber man stuck the soles of his feet to the back of his locks and walked on his hands. Then the local calypso-reggae trio, who called themselves the Pioneers, sang a few Bob Marley songs while the diners ate veal and red snapper. When the band shifted into a perfect, crystalline version of the old mento "Yellow Bird," all eating stopped as the music took hold. By the time the trio got through the heartbreaking "If I Had the Wings of a Dove," the women were crying and the men were wiping their eyes with their napkins.

The persistent reference you hear in Jamaica is to the country's adolescence. Like any fifteen-year-old Jamaica is rambunctious and aggressive, and also sullen and withdrawn. People say, "It's a bad time" like

Don Topping

they're talking about a young delinquent who's eventually expected to pull himself together, solve his own problems, and grow up.

At this writing, the future of Jamaican music is still up for grabs. The Wailers and the Maytals are making it, and dozens more are hanging out in Kingston, waiting for the main chance. One indication of reggae's future lies with its women. For years female singers have been in the background of reggae, and only recently are they starting to move up front. Rita Marley has written some of the Wailers' best tunes. Judy Mowatt's dusky voice has yet to reach its great potential. Marcia Griffiths has a disquieting, mysterious style that can't fail to catch on if properly produced. Joy White's 1974 "C'mon Natty Dread" marked the first time a woman had embraced Rastafari in song, and started a trend that's still growing. Lorna Bennett, who recorded the great "Breakfast in Bed," will undoubtedly be heard from again.

Since 1969, reggae has slowed somewhat, almost imperceptibly, in its basic rhythm, probably due to orthodox Rasta drumming. But lately the pace has begun to pick up again with producer Bunny Lee's "flying cymbal" rhythms (called "rockers"). The latest trend (at the end of 1976) is the "militant beat," worked out primarily by drummer Carlie "Sly" Dunbar of the Skin Flesh and Bone band. "Militant" drumming features the bass drum four to the bar and much busier snare work. At the same time ska, rock-steady, early reggae forms, and all the "riddims" now coexist in the Kingston studios in various permutations and cross-pollinations. Reggae is moving faster than anyone can keep up with it.

Postscript: Heavy Manners

The sociopolitical hurricane that is buffeting Jamaica came to a climax at the end of 1976. In November the Manley government announced that general elections would be held in December, and the Jamaican people would be given another chance to decide between Manleyan socialism and the right-wing conservatism of the opposition. Despite the state of emergency that the government had declared the previous June, the campaign was bitterly violent. A Jamaica Labor Party motorcade was fired upon while touring the country. A People's National Party candidate was gunned down while campaigning in a Kingston shopping center. Dozens of stabbings and beatings drove the rhetoric to strange heights of frenzy. The opposition carried on its usual red-baiting. A vote for Manley, it said, was a vote for communism in Jamaica. Manley counterattacked with ominous warnings of the Labor Party's involvement with what he called the destabilization of the country. And even the disinterested observer could see that in a country the size of Jamaica it wouldn't take a lot of destabilizing to bring the government down; perhaps only a boatload of guns or counterfeit currency deposited on the North Coast on a moonless night could do it if the conditions were right.

Naturally, reggae played a part in the campaign. Lord Larrow, a Trinadadian musician living in Jamaica, released a wonderful single called "Foreign Press," which echoed the Manley line that negative reports about Jamaica in British and American newspapers were part of the general climate of destabilization and nation-wrecking. Once again Delroy Wilson was called on for a campaign theme song and came up with "Heavy Manners," which was also the PNP election slogan. The

phrase "under heavy manners" in Jamaica describes a child being disciplined by its parents. Michael Manley's state of emergency, his rule-by-decree, and his government's economic austerity measures effectively put the entire Jamaican people under heavy manners. The implication was that national discipline was necessary for the survival of the nation, and the choice for voters was clear.

Bob Marley was even pressured to lay aside his Rasta anarchism and declare for the government and socialism. Marley and the Wailers agreed to appear with Michael Manley at a mass rally and free concert, co-sponsored by the government, at the Kingston racecourse a week before the election. The concert—nominally unpolitical—was to be called *Smile Jamaica,* stressing national unity and harmony. The Wailers went into the studio and released a single called "Smile Jamaica," with Bob Marley scat-singing vibrantly as the great band burned away behind him.

On December 3, three days before the concert, the Wailers were rehearsing in the little recording studio behind Marley's house on Hope Road. The whole band was there with its families and hangers-on. While the Wailers were relaxing during a break, two white Toyota sedans pulled into the gateway. One blocked the entrance while the second roared into the front yard. Four men armed with submachine guns and automatic pistols got out of the car and began blasting at the house. A bullet fired point-blank grazed Rita Marley's head as she tried to escape out a side door with five children in tow. One of the gunmen, a very young and jittery kid of about sixteen, ran into the little kitchen of the studio and pointed his weapon at Bob Marley and sprayed. One bullet grazed the singer's heart; another pierced his right arm. Don Taylor, Marley's manager, was between the gun and Marley and took five bullets in the groin. A friend of the band who was in the room was also seriously injured. Family Man and a dozen others crowded into the toilet and locked the door.

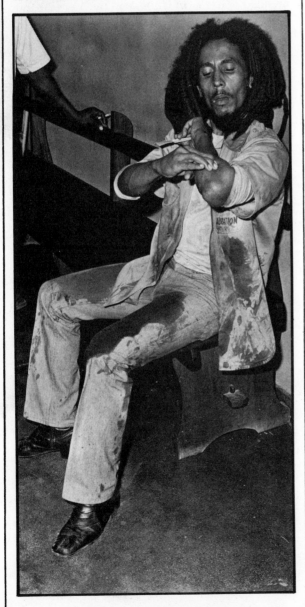

The bullet hit Marley's left arm

A patrolling police car routed the intruders but was mysteriously unable to capture them. Miraculously, no one was killed. Marley and his wife were treated for their wounds and released. Don Taylor was flown to a hospital in Miami. No one knew why the house had been attacked, though it was widely assumed that the shooting was the work of a JLP goon squad seeking to stop the free concert. There were also responsible observers who suggested that the government might have engineered the near-killings to gain the inevitable anti-JLP backlash. And there were possibly accurate rumors in the Kingstonian demimonde that the attack was the work of Jamaican gangland. One of Bob Marley's closest friends had been involved with a racetrack scandal and fled the country with half a million dollars. It was postulated that, since the thugs couldn't put their hands on Marley's friend, Marley himself was set up in revenge. Whatever the scenario, the shooting was amateurish and Marley went into hiding.

He did emerge three days later. The concert went on as scheduled, and Bob and Rita Marley sang wrapped in bandages in front of fifty thousand Jamaicans. Michael Manley spoke and the Wailers played for an hour. When the concert was over, the fifty thousand vanished very quickly. Nobody knew what was going on, the vibes were weird, and nobody was going to hang around. Witnesses swore they never saw a crowd disassemble so fast.

The election on December 15 was supposed to be close. Instead the Manley government won forty-eight out of the sixty seats in Parliament, an astounding mandate for socialism in Jamaica. Bob Marley, convinced that unseen forces were trying to kill him, took his family and left the island. If you asked where he was, you were told that he was incognito, somewhere in the Caribbean.

S.D.
Massachusetts
Feb. 1977

Further Reading

The literature of reggae is slim. Carl Gayle, of *Black Music* magazine, is the quintessential reggae writer; his journalism is an invaluable source for anyone interested not only in reggae but in any kind of music. A rare pamphlet, "Reggae: A People's Music," by Rolston Kallyndyr and Henderson Dalrymple (Carib-Arawak Publications, London, 1973), is helpful in putting modern Jamaican music in perspective. Michael Thomas' and Adrian Boot's *Babylon on a Thin Wire* (Thames and Hudson, London, 1976; Schocken Books, Inc., New York, 1977) focuses on Jamaica's darker side in the traditions of gonzo journalism.

The prime printed source on the Brotherhood of Rastafari is the "Report on the Rastafari Movement in Kingston, Jamaica," a pamphlet by Rex Nettleford, M. G. Smith, and Roy Augier (Institute of Social and Economic Research, University of the West Indies, Kingston, 1960). Rex Nettleford's excellent *Mirror Mirror—Identity, Race and Protest in Jamaica* (Collins and Sangster, Kingston, 1970) is the most concise analysis of modern Jamaica available.

An excellent study of Rastafarianism in Kingston was recently published in Kingston by Joseph Owens, a Jesuit priest who approaches his subject with sympathy and fascination. The book is called "Dread—The Rastafarians of Jamaica" (Sangster, Kingston, 1976) and is causing a lot of people in Jamaica to get religious and re-examine accepted history.

For a detailed portrait of Marcus Garvey, E. D. Cronon's *Black Moses* (University of Wisconsin Press, Madison, 1966) is recommended. *Ganja in Jamaica,* by Vera Rubin and Lambros Comitas (Anchor Press/Doubleday, New York, 1976), is the fascinating report of recent research by the Research Institute for the Study of Man. Carey Robinson's *The Fighting Maroons of Jamaica* (Collins and Sangster, Kingston, 1969) is the most accessible work on the history of the Jamaican Maroons. Also worthwhile is *Maroon Societies—Rebel Slave Communities in the Americas,* Richard Price, ed. (Anchor Press, Garden City, 1973).

Wonderful reading can also be found in *Jamaican Anansi Stories,* by Martha Warren Beckwith (American Folklore Society, New York, 1924). Also useful is Helen Roberts' essay, "Possible Survivals of African Song in Jamaica," published in *Musical Quarterly,* July 1926.

Jamaica Discography

— Compiled by Don Williams —

BIG YOUTH

RECORD LABEL	RECORD NO.	ALBUM TITLE
Trojan	TRLS 61	Screaming Target (U.K. import)
Trojan	TRLS 123	Natty Cultural Dread (U.K. import)
TR International	——	Dread Locks Dread (Jamaican import)
Negusa Nagast	003	Hit the Road Jack! (Jamaican import)

BOB ANDY & MARCIA GRIFFITHS

Trojan	TRLS 26	Pied Piper (U.K. import)
Trojan	TBL 122	Young, Gifted & Black (U.K. import)

KEN BOOTH

Wildflower	XYZ 001	Mr. Booth (Jamaican import)
Federal	FRM 135	Booth Unlimited (Jamaican import)
Trojan	TRLS 58	Black, Gold & Green (U.K. import)
Trojan	TRLS 95	Everything I Own (U.K. import)
Trojan	TRLS 83	Let's Get It On (U.K. import)

BURNING SPEAR

Studio One		Burning Spear (Jamaican import)
Studio One	SOL 1123	Rocking Time (Jamaican import)
Island	ILPS 9377	Marcus Garvey
Island	ILPS 9382	Garvey's Ghost (dub)
Island	ILPS 9412	Man in the Hills
Mango	MLPS 9431	Dry & Heavy

JIMMY CLIFF

Veep	VPS 16536	Can't Get Enough of It
A & M	SP 4251	Wonderful World Beautiful People
Island	ILPS 9159	Another Cycle (U.K. import)
Island	ILPS 9235	Struggling Man
Mango	9202	Harder They Come
Island	ICD-6	Best of Jimy Cliff (U.K. import)
Warner Bros.	MS 2147	Unlimited
Warner Bros.	MS 2188	Music Maker
Warner Bros.	MS 2218	Follow My Mind
Warner Bros.	MS 2256	In Concert the Best of Jimmy Cliff

DESMOND DEKKER

Trojan	TBL 146	You Can Get It if You Really Want (U.K. import)

RECORD LABEL	RECORD NO.	ALBUM TITLE
Trojan	TBL-153	This Is Desmond Dekker (U.K. import)
Trojan	TRLD-401	Double Dekker (U.K. import)
Uni	73059	Israelites

DILLINGER

Mango	MLPS 9385	CB 200

ERIC DONALDSON

Trojan	TRL 42	Eric Donaldson (U.K. import)

ERIC GALE

Micron	2096	Negril (Jamaican import)

OWEN GRAY

Total Sounds	——	Forward on the Scene (Jamaican import)

HEPTONES

Studio One	——	Heptones (Jamaican import)
Studio One	——	Heptones on Top (Jamaican import)
Studio One	——	Freedom Line (Jamaican import)
Trojan	TBL 183	Heptones & Their Friends (U.K. import)
Island	ILPS 9297	Book of Rules (U.K. import)
Island	ILPS 9381	Nightfood

JOE HIGGS

Groundation	GROL 508	Life of Contradiction (U.K. import)

JUSTIN HINES AND THE DOMINOES

Island	ILPS 9416	Jezebel

JOHN HOLT

Trojan	TRLS 37	Still in Chains (U.K. import)
Trojan	TRLS 43	Holt (U.K. import)
Trojan	TRLS 55	The Further You Look (U.K. import)
Trojan	TRLS 75	One Thousand Volts of Holt (U.K. import)
Trojan	TRLS 85	Dusty Roads (U.K. import)
Trojan	TBL 184	Pledging My Love (U.K. import)

JAH LION

Island	ILPS 9386	Colombia Colly (U.K. import)

BYRON LEE AND THE DRAGONAIRES

Trojan	TRLS 5	Rock Steady Explosion (U.K. import)

RECORD LABEL	RECORD NO.	ALBUM TITLE
Trojan	TRLS 8	Sparrow Meets the Dragon (U.K. import)
Trojan	TRLS 18	Reggae
Trojan	TRLS 28	Reggay Splash Down! (U.K. import)
Trojan	TRLS 40	Reggay Hot and Cool and Easy (U.K. import)
Trojan	TBL 110	Reggae Blast Off (U.K. import)

BOB MARLEY & THE WAILERS

Coxsone	——	The Wailing Wailers (Jamaican import)
Coxsone	——	Best of Bob Marley & the Wailers (Jamaican import)
Upsetter	——	Soul Revolution—Part I (Jamaican import)
Upsetter	——	Soul Revolution—Part II (Jamaican import)
Trojan	TBL 127	Soul Rebels (U.K. import)
Beverlys	BLP 001	Best of the Wailers (Jamaican import)
Trojan	TRLS 62	African Herdsman (U.K. import)
Trojan	TRLS 89	Rasta Revolution (U.K. import)
Island	ILPS 9241	Catch a Fire
Island	ILPS 9256	Burnin'
Island	ILPS 9281	Natty Dread
Island	ILPS 9376	Wailers Live
Island	ILPS 9383	Rastaman Vibration
Calla	2CAS-1240	The Birth of a Legend
Island	ILPS 9498	Exodus

TOMMY MCCOOK

Trojan	TBL 111	Greater Jamaica (U.K. import)

MIGHTY DIAMONDS

Virgin	PZ 34235	Right Time
Virgin	PZ 34454	Ice On Fire

J. R. MURVIN

Island	MLPS 9499	Police & Thieves

JOHNNY NASH

Jadd	J 1007	Hold Me Tight
Epic	KE 31607	I Can See Clearly
CBS	69097	Greatest Hits (U.K. import)

COUNT OSSIE AND THE MYSTIC REVELATION OF RASTAFARI

Groundation	NTI 301	Count Ossie & the Mystic Revelation of Rastafari (Jamaican import)

RECORD LABEL	RECORD NO.	ALBUM TITLE
THE PIONEERS		
Trojan	TRLS 24	Let Your Yeah Be Yeah (U.K. import)
Trojan	TRLS 48	I Believe in Love (U.K. import)
Trojan	TRLS 64	Freedom Feeling (U.K. import)
Trojan	TBL 103	Longshot (U.K. import)
Trojan	TBL 139	Battle of the Giants (U.K. import)
PLUTO		
Wildflower	XYZ 006	Greatest Hits (Jamaican import)
Wildflower	LP 366	Ramgoat (Jamaican import)
Wildflower	LP 373	Pluto (Jamaican import)
Wildflower	LP 3779	Playmas (Jamaican import)
THE PROPHETS		
Micron	——	Conquering Lion (Jamaican import)
RAS MICHAEL AND THE SONS OF NEGUS		
Talent Corporation	—	Rastafari (Jamaican import)
Dynamic	DYP 3004	Freedom Sounds
Trojan	TRLS 132	Tribute to the Emperor
MAX ROMEO		
Island	ILPS 9465	Reconstruction
I ROY		
Trojan	TRLS 63	Presenting I Roy (U.K. import)
Trojan	TRLS 71	Hell & Sorrow (U.K. import)
Trojan	TRLS 91	Many Moods of I Roy (U.K. import)
Trojan	TBL 161	Version Galore (U.K. import)
Attack	ATLP 1006	I Roy
Micron	——	Truth and Rights (Jamaican import)
Virgin	——	Crisis Time (U.K. import)
ERNIE SMITH		
Federal	FLD JA 160	Greatest Hits (Jamaican import)
Federal	347	Ernie (Jamaican import)
Federal	356	For the Good Times (Jamaican import)
Wildflower	LP 369	I'll Sing for Jesus (Jamaican import)
Wildflower	377	Pure Gold Rock Steady (Jamaican import)
Trojan	TRLS 79	Life Is Just for Living (U.K. import)
THIRD WORLD		
Island	ILPS 9369	Third World

RECORD LABEL	RECORD NO.	ALBUM TITLE
Island	ILPS 9443	Third World

NICKY THOMAS

Trojan	TRLS 25	Tell It Like It Is (U.K. import)
Trojan	TBL 143	Love of the Common People (U.K. import)

TOOTS & THE MAYTALS

Coxsone	JBL 1113	Never Grow Old (Jamaican import)
Dynamic	B/LP 003	The Sensational Maytals (Jamaican import)
Trojan	TRLS 65	From the Roots (U.K. import)
Trojan	TBL 107	Monkey Man (U.K. import)
Dynamic	DY 331	Slatyam Stoot (Jamaican import)
Island	ILPS 9330	Funky Kingston
Island	ILPS 9231	In the Dark (U.K. import)
Island	ILPS 9374	Reggae Got Soul

PETER TOSH

Columbia	PC 34253	Legalize It
Columbia	PC34670	Equal Rights

UPSETTERS

Trojan	TRL 19	Return of Django (U.K. import)
Trojan	TRLS 70	Double Seven (U.K. import)
Trojan	TBL 119	The Good, the Bad, and the Upsetter (U.K. import)
Trojan	TBL 125	Eastwood Rides Again (U.K. import)
Island	ILPS 9417	Super Ape

U ROY

Trojan	TBL 161	Version Galore (U.K. import)
Virgin	PZ 34234	Dread in a Babylon

BUNNY WAILER

Island	ILPS 9415	Blackheart Man

DELROY WILSON

Trojan	TBL 44	Bettah Must Come (U.K. import)
Jaguar	——	Greatest Hits (Jamaican import)

ZAP POW

Harry J. Records	——	Revolutionary (Jamaican import)

VARIOUS ARTISTS

Trojan	TBL 120	Tighten Up (U.K. import)
Trojan	TBL 131	Tighten Up, Vol. 2 (U.K. import)
Trojan	TBL 145	Tighten Up, Vol. 3 (U.K. import)
Trojan	TBL 163	Tighten Up, Vol. 4 (U.K. import)

RECORD LABEL	RECORD NO.	ALBUM TITLE
Trojan	TBL 164	Club Reggae, Vol. 2 (U.K. import)
Trojan	TBL 166	Africa's Blood (U.K. import)
Trojan	TBL 169	Reggae Chartbusters, Vol. 3 (U.K. import)
Trojan	TBL 175	Version Galore, Vol. 2 (U.K. import)
Trojan	TBL 178	Club Reggae, Vol. 3 (U.K. import)
Trojan	TBL 180	Trojan's Greatest Hits, Vol. 1 (U.K. import)
Trojan	TBL 181	Reggae Jamaica, Vol. 2 (U.K. import)
Trojan	TBL 182	Version to Version (U.K. import)
Trojan	TBL 188	Club Reggae, Vol. 4 (U.K. import)
Trojan	TBL 190	Trojan's Greatest Hits, Vol. 2 (U.K. import)
Trojan	TBL 193	Reggae Jamaica, Vol. 1 (U.K. import)
Trojan	TBL 200	Version Galore, Vol. 3 (U.K. import)
Trojan	TBL 201	Charmers in Session (U.K. import)
Trojan	TBL 203	Pipeline (U.K. import)
Trojan	TBL 204	Reggae Jamaica, Vol. 3 (U.K. import)
Trojan	TBL 206	Version to Version, Vol. 3 (U.K. import)
Trojan	TBL 207	Tighten Up, Vol. 8 (U.K. import)
Trojan	TBL 208	Trojan's Greatest Hits, Vol. 3
Trojan	TBL 209	16 Dynamic Reggae Hits (U.K. import)
Mango	MLPS-9202	The Harder They Come
Trojan	TALL-1	Trojan History
Island	Vol. I ILPS 9251	This Is Reggae Music
	Vol. II ILPS 9327	This Is Reggae Music
	Vol. III ILPS 9391	This is Reggae Music
*Columbia House	1P 6298	Feelin' High
Shelter	SRL 52023	Roots

*Available through Columbia House mail order only.

Stephen Davis is a well-known writer and journalist whose work has appeared in a wide variety of newspapers and magazines. He is a former associate editor of *Rolling Stone,* has done field recordings of tribal music in North Africa for the National Geographic Society, and is working on a novel about Morocco.

Peter Simon's photographs have appeared in *Life, Rolling Stone,* the New York *Times,* and numerous other magazines and books. His work has been the subject of one-man shows in galleries in New York, Boston, and San Francisco. His books include *Moving On, Holding Still* (1972), *Decent Exposures* (1974), and *Carly Simon Complete* (1975).